What students are saying:

"I only wish I had started working with them sooner because they're amazing. Very prompt responses, and qualified people to make your application the best it can be. Don't wait like me just a few weeks into the application cycle to work with them, there's a lot they can help you with before so that the experience is as least stressful as possible." — PreMak

"Very helpful! Excellent job, 5 stars for all my reviewers. Thorough and quick review, with detailed comments and advice, guidelines, rules of thumb, and I really appreciate that they fit my schedule and is [sic] asynchronous." — Grace

"BeMo has been excellent every step of the way throughout the application process. They gave incisive feedback that polished all of my essays and application materials. I am extremely grateful for BeMo, and I think their work will definitely help me in the long run." — Dawson

"I was pretty confused on the general application process but the first brainstorming session with Joseph really helped clear the air on how it works, what is required, and further steps to get ready for my personal deadline on when to apply." — Syed

"I am a re-applicant and in working with BeMo for both my primary and starting my secondary applications, I can note the significant improvement from last year. My brainstorming session was very thorough but efficient. BeMo's consultants are very helpful and knowledgeable." — Matthew

"Quick responses, incredibly helpful guidance for my applications. Thank you, BeMo!" — Ari

"I am very thankful that I chose to work with BeMo. They have unquestionably increased the quality of my application and essays and have a number of resources which have supported me in various ways. Most of the experts that I have worked with have been helpful and offered great insight." — Customer

"I'm still in the process of the application so I'm not sure how much BeMo can help me in terms of increasing my chance of getting in. But my experience up to now showed that they have really fast response time and their reviews of the application materials are detailed and helpful." — Ho

"Aali was an excellent listener and it felt like he really understood the areas that I was struggling with. He provided specific and actionable feedback in a kind manner and it has helped me a great deal. Would highly recommend Aali to anyone!" — Customer

"BeMo's application services have been extremely helpful so far! The counsellors have been providing valuable feedback on my written submissions, which has been really helpful as a new applicant." — Customer

"I spoke with Dr. Arora. First of all, he is very kind and wants you to succeed. He gave me some important advice with my responses and at the same time really pointed out my strengths. Really easy to speak with and a wonderful experience." — Michael

"Dr. Malhotra was very thorough in her explanations and helped me approach the questions in a more organized manner. She made sure that I understood what she was trying to explain before moving onto the next question and I never felt rushed during the session." — Customer

"Wonderful experience working with experts who are well versed in any facet of the application process." — Orestes

"I received a lot of constructive feedback on the documents I had submitted. The greatest perk of this program is that the reviewers provide extensive feedback/revision to all documents within a short amount of time. They make an effort to state not only your weaknesses but also your strengths in each document which feels much more motivating during each round of revision." — Customer

"My consultant, Dr. Poirier, helped me construct and build upon my thoughts to ensure my responses were good, concise, and to the point with personal experiences. Walking through each question thoroughly and getting to know what I need to work on and have improved on has really helped me. Thank you!" — Customer

"My academic counsellor gave clear feedback and answered all my questions about my application in great detail. Appreciate their input and help!" — Customer

"Dr. Ketelyn did such a great job at breaking down the different types of questions and how they should all be approached. She made me aware of strategies I wasn't aware of before, and how to use questions that initially seemed difficult to show my strengths and how I would contribute to the program of interest." — Daniel

"Benita was extremely helpful in helping craft my personal narrative. She was reassuring and able to take my experiences to help me outline a personal statement that will impress any admissions committee." — Customer

"Emily Giroux was my consultant during the personal statement brainstorming session. She was very helpful in suggesting ideas and organizing my thoughts. The most beneficial part was how I can address my gaps appropriately." — Customer

"I just wanted to express my sincere gratitude for the excellent editing work Christine did on my personal statement. Christine's attention to detail and constructive feedback were exactly what I needed to take my essay to the next level." — Customer

BeMo's Ultimate Guide to Ivy League College Essays & Personal Statements

How to Write Captivating Essays and Statements Even If You Are Not a Natural Writer

BeMo® Academic Consulting Inc.

ISBN 13: 9798375792965

CONTRIBUTING AUTHORS

Dr. Behrouz Moemeni, Ph.D., founder & CEO of BeMo

Ms. Ronza Nissan, M.A., admissions expert & lead trainer

Dr. Shaheen Anis, Ph.D., admissions expert

Dr. Martin Poirier, Ph.D., admissions expert

Ms. Vicky Cerdeira, M.S., admissions expert

Ms. Sophia Xian, B.S., admissions expert

Ms. Andrea Grainger, B.A., book publication manager

EDITOR

Ms. Andrea Grainger, B.A., book publication manager

Would you like us to help you make your applications stand out?

Go to
BeMoUndergrad.com

To Schedule Your FREE Initial Consultation Now!

Contents

Acknowledgments

We would like to thank our students and their parents for putting their trust in us and giving us the privilege of being a part of their journey. You have inspired us and taught us lessons we would not have learned on our own. Thank you for your continued support and for investing in our mission. You are the reason we get up in the morning.

We would like to thank the countless number of admissions deans, directors, officers, and school counselors who have 'unofficially' supported our mission. Thank you for encouraging us and, most importantly, thank you for making us think critically. We appreciate what you do, and we understand the impossible task you face every day.

A huge thanks to our team members, both past and present. BeMo wouldn't be what it is today without you.

And, of course, a huge thanks to our family and friends who have been unconditionally supportive, even when we couldn't spend as much time with them because of our obsession with our mission here at BeMo.

Foreword

First, CONGRATULATIONS for making the commitment to educate yourself on becoming not only a competitive applicant but a better person and a better future professional. The fact that you have purchased this book tells us that you understand the value of continuous learning and self-improvement. The world rewards individuals who continuously seek to educate themselves because *knowledge is power*. Before we dive in, let's get on the same page about the purpose of this book, who this book is for, who it is NOT for, and why you should listen to us. But first, a few words from our founder and CEO, Behrouz Moemeni.

Why I founded BeMo®: A message from BeMo's founder and CEO, Dr. Behrouz Moemeni

Sometimes you must do what's necessary, even if the chances of success are slim to none. Students often ask me what gets me up in the morning and what motivated me to found BeMo. The answer is rather simple and has been since day one.

I started BeMo with my cofounder, Dr. Mo Bayegan, in 2013 — see why it's called "BeMo" now? Our partnership started when we first met back in high school in 1996, and then later solidified during our undergraduate and graduate training years.

We both felt every student deserves access to higher education, regardless of their social status or cultural background, because education is the best way to introduce positive change in our world.

Sadly, I believe most of the current admissions practices, tools, and procedures are biased, outdated, and, more importantly, scientifically unproven. Therefore, in 2013, as Mo and I were finishing our graduate studies, we decided to create BeMo to make sure no one is treated unfairly due to flawed admissions practices.

At the time, I was finishing my Ph.D. studies in Immunology at the University of Toronto, which was a transformational educational experience. I had the privilege of working with one of the sharpest minds in the field, Dr. Michael Julius. He taught me many things over the years, but two lessons stayed with me: 1) There is tremendous value in having curiosity in scientific or technological innovations to seek the truth, rather than confirming one's own opinions, and 2) whatever you do has to be the reason that gets you up in the morning. Though I wasn't his best student, I was still relatively successful. During my Ph.D., I won 19 awards, was invited to seven international conferences, and even had an unsolicited job offer before I had defended my thesis. The job offered a secure source of income, and I would have been able to start paying my mounting student loan debt. However, I decided to abandon a career in academia in favor of starting BeMo. Despite the uncertainty, the existence of many well-established competitors, and the lack of a secure source of income, I felt, and still do to this day, that the mission was well worth the risk, even if the probability of success seemed infinitely slim. I truly believe what we do here at BeMo adds more value to our students' lives than anything else I could have done, and I would not trade it for the world.

Over the years, our amazing and steadily growing team has helped many students navigate the admissions process. We really couldn't have done it without them, and it's been a privilege to teach with them and learn from them over the years. (Thanks for sticking with us!)

We are aware that our methods have been controversial in some circles; innovative ideas often are. However, we are confident in our belief — and the scientific literature supports this — that current admissions practices are rife with bias and must be improved.

This is why, in 2017, I founded another independent company called SortSmart®, which has created what I consider to be the fairest, most scientifically sound, and cost-effective admissions screening tool out there. I invite you to visit SortSmart.com to learn more and tell your university admissions office to bring SortSmart to your school.

In the meantime, while SortSmart is gathering momentum, at BeMo, we will continue to support students just like you to make sure no groups of students are treated unfairly. You can rest assured that we will not stop until our goals have been achieved.

To your success,
Behrouz Moemeni, Ph.D.
CEO @ BeMo

A bit about us: BeMo Academic Consulting (BeMo)

We are an energetic academic consulting firm, comprised of a team of researchers and professionals who use a proven, evidence-based, and scientific approach to help prospective students with career path development and admissions to undergraduate, graduate, and professional programs, such as medicine, law, dentistry, and pharmacy.

We believe your education is one of your most valuable assets and learning how to become a great future professional or scholar doesn't need to be complicated. We also believe that every student deserves access to higher education, regardless of their social status or cultural background. However, in our opinion, most of the current admissions practices, tools, and procedures are biased, outdated, and, more importantly, scientifically unproven.

Our goal is to create truly useful (and scientifically sound) programs and tools that work and provide more than just trivial information like the other admissions consulting companies out there. We want to make sure everyone has a fair chance of admission to highly competitive professional programs despite current biases in admissions practices.

We do whatever it takes to generate creative solutions and then test them like mad scientists. We're passionate about mentoring our students. We're obsessed with delivering useful educational programs, and we go where others dare not to explore.

Why should you listen to us?

We are the leaders in admission preparation for extremely competitive professional schools. Each year, we help thousands of students gain admission to top schools around the world by assisting them with their application documents and preparing them for interviews of all styles, including traditional interviews and video interviews. We have an exceptional team of practicing professionals, doctors, scholars, and scientists who have served as former admissions committee members. (You can learn more about our experts by visiting our website at BeMoAcademicConsulting.com). What we are about to share with you in this book is based on what we learned in our sought-after paid training programs. What we offer works, and it works consistently. In fact, research has shown that our programs can increase application scores by up to 27%. Our programs are in high demand, and we are certain they will also work for you.

Why did we write this book?

There is so much misinformation about the admissions process, both online and offline — from online forums to university clubs, and even some university guidance counselors and official test administrators. While some of this information is well-intended, the level of inaccuracy is astounding. In particular, the credibility of most online forums can be called into question because it is not clear who the authors are or what their motivations are. These forums are frequently filled with fake profiles, some of them official university administrators and test administrators trying to control the flow of information so only their version of 'facts' is distributed. To make matters worse, some of these forums offer sponsorship opportunities to companies, which puts them in a financial conflict of interest. Also, be wary of information from most student clubs. These organizations frequently form financial relationships with companies to garner support for their operations and, as such, they receive and distribute one-sided information. Additionally, most books available are incomplete and tend to focus on teaching you 'tricks' about applications, without offering a systematic strategy on how to write an effective personal statement. They do not focus on the big picture that is essential to your success, both as an applicant and as a future practicing professional.

What is this book about?

This book is about the big picture: how to capture your journey in words. We spend a considerable amount of time walking you through specific instructions on how to write well-articulated and effective personal statements and supplemental essays, while helping you to remain focused on the big question: Why do you want to pursue Ivy League studies?

Who is this book for and who is it NOT for?

If you are applying to any program that requires you to submit essays, then this book is perfect for you. Regardless of where you are currently with your application, whether you have already started the writing process or have yet to devote time to thinking about it, this book has something for you, provided that you are willing to put in the hard work and invest in yourself. Getting into a competitive professional school is challenging, as is becoming a practicing professional. In fact, the journey is both very difficult and very consuming of your time, money, and energy. We do NOT share any quick 'tricks,' 'shortcuts,' or 'insider scoops' like some of the other books you may find. Therefore, this book is NOT for anyone who is looking for an easy, cheap shortcut to get in.

We do not share any such tricks or shortcuts because:

A) You cannot trick your way into becoming a mature, ethical professional. Rather, you must put in long hours of self-training. Think of it this way: If a professional athlete must train for years – on average ten years, hence the 'ten-year rule' – to get to that level of proficiency, wouldn't it make sense that our future doctors, lawyers, dentists, pharmacists, and other professionals would need to put in the effort to learn the necessary skills?

B) Sharing 'tricks' or 'insider scoops' would be highly unethical. You should be immediately alarmed if a book or admissions company claims to be sharing 'insider' information.

C) We have a strict policy at BeMo to only help students who are genuinely interested in becoming caring future professionals who want to help their community, rather than those who may be primarily motivated by financial security, status, or social pressure from their parents and peers.

How should you read this book?

We recommend that you first read this book cover to cover, and then return to specific chapters for a detailed read. The more you read it, the more you will internalize the essential strategies. It is important to note that there is a lot of information in this book, and if you try to do everything at once, it may be overwhelming and lead to discouragement. Therefore, it is best that you first read this book for pleasure from cover to cover, and then gradually start to implement our recommendations.

To your success,
Your friends at BeMo

CHAPTER I

Why Do We Write Personal Statements?

One of the key components of any Ivy League application is the personal statement (also called a personal essay, application essay, or essay), which is why it must be approached with intention and care. To help you write an outstanding personal statement, we first need to look at the rationale behind using them.

The rationale behind personal statements

Ivy League applications may consist of *some or all* of the following: a copy of your high school transcript or grades, a list of your activities (including work and family responsibilities), CV or resume, college entrance exam test scores (e.g., ACT, SAT), academic honors and achievements, personal statement, supplemental essays (such as college-specific essays or written supplements), letters of recommendation, and interview performance. A prospective Ivy League student may wonder why schools ask for a personal statement during the application process. After all, don't admissions committees find out enough about you from your transcript, college entrance exam test scores, and letters of recommendation?

Ivy League schools ask for a personal statement because they believe this document provides insight into your life experiences, your motivations for pursuing a field of study, and your ability to communicate effectively through writing. They claim that personal statements can reveal your professional skills, attributes, and abilities, such as collaborative skills, leadership potential, and empathy. Furthermore, personal statements can surface potential 'red flags,' such as poor written communication skills, dubious ethical decision-making, or lack of professionalism. However, such claims have not been proven by any form of research. Personal statements have not been shown to provide any valuable information about the suitability of applicants for a profession. Rather, they have been shown to cause profound bias against certain applicants based on race, culture, and socioeconomic status. Sadly, this is also true for assessments based on transcripts or grades and college entrance exam test scores. This is why, at BeMo, we want to level the playing field. We believe everyone with the right motivations deserves access to higher education.

Regardless of the effectiveness of personal statements for candidate selection, you may be wondering *why* Ivy League schools want to know anything about your personal abilities, skills, and traits. Ivy League schools are academically rigorous, so why isn't it enough that you have already achieved excellent grades and high college entrance exam test scores?

The reality of most professions is that they encompass much more than learning a vast amount of technical knowledge. Any professional is also an empathetic communicator, a role model, a teacher, and a leader in their community. Great trust is placed in professionals to be responsible in their duties. Therefore, Ivy League schools must ensure that their students are not only intellectually capable, but also mature, thoughtful, and trustworthy. While transcripts or grades and college entrance exam test scores can convey some of this information, programs have opted to dig deeper and seek out additional information from candidates through various avenues, including the personal statement.

What do Ivy League schools ask you to write in your personal statement? The answer varies. When Ivy League schools ask you to submit a personal statement, they provide specific essay prompts in the application system. All eight Ivy League schools use Common App, but some also accept applications through QuestBridge or Coalition App. We recommend using an application system that partners with all the schools where you plan to apply. Since Common App is used by all the Ivy League schools, it is a good option (and it is the application system reflected in this book). You will find more details about the prompts you may encounter in Common App later in this chapter, which are similar to the QuestBridge and Coalition App prompts.

When you are beginning to prepare your application, ask yourself the following questions:

- Why are you interested in a particular profession?

- When did you first realize you wanted to pursue the profession?

- What experiences did you seek to confirm your desire to pursue the profession? For example, you can mention volunteering, teaching or tutoring, extracurricular activities, or any other relevant experience.

- What traits, skills, and abilities do you possess that might help you to be effective in the profession? Are you a good communicator, an empathetic teacher, a reliable professional, and a critical thinker?

- What experiences have you had that led you to develop the above traits?

- What do you know about the profession and the challenges you may face as you navigate your education?

- What are your future plans with your degree?

Thinking through these points will allow you to begin considering some of the experiences and abilities you may want to highlight in your essay. It is important to show admissions committees that you have thoughtfully chosen a career to pursue and sought experiences that have allowed you to develop the skills that a successful professional possesses.

The importance of the personal statement means you must devote time and thought into making it cohesive, effective, and powerful. This is not a task that can be left until the last minute, and it should not be rushed. An effective personal statement can take several weeks – even months – to draft, revise, and submit. This means you should begin planning your writing process at least 6 to 8 weeks before the application process begins. You must be prepared to submit your application, including the completed personal statement, as soon as the systems open, which is typically in July or August of each year. You must begin to look at personal statements as a key component that schools will use to determine whether they will grant you acceptance into their program.

The rationale behind essay prompts

Ivy League schools provide essay prompts for you to answer through application systems such as Common App, QuestBridge, and Coalition App. These can be quite similar to the essay prompts discussed below. Regardless of the application system you use, individual Ivy League schools may have additional writing requirements, which is why we recommend using BeMo's expert services to guide you through your application process.

Besides a personal statement, you may be required to write supplemental essays. Why do you need to write more essays in addition to your personal statement? Is the personal statement not enough? The main purpose of supplemental essays is to determine if you are a good fit with the mission and values of the program and with the overall ethos of the institution. Essentially, Ivy League schools want to dig deeper on the ideas you addressed in your personal statement and find out whether you will make not just a great professional, but one who fits into their program. Additionally, Ivy League schools seek out additional essays to further assess each applicant's personal characteristics, expanding on the traits highlighted in other parts of the application, such as your personal statement, activities, and letters of recommendation.

Luckily, you can prepare for your personal statement and supplemental essays in advance to manage your time more effectively. Many schools pose questions similar to those asked during previous application cycles, and you can create a list of common themes that you will likely have to address during the essay writing process. You can then create outlines or rough drafts of essays that address each of these themes. Pre-planning these essays will help you be efficient in your writing and prevent the feeling of being overwhelmed.

Common themes you can prepare for in advance include:

- Reasons why you are applying to a specific program
- Cultural competency and diversity
- Overcoming challenges
- Career goals and aspirations
- Explaining academic lapses or breaks in your studies
- If you have already graduated, what you have been doing since graduation
- What you would like the reviewers to know about you that was not already covered

These themes are further discussed below.

Why are you interested in our program?

To answer this question, you must first ensure that you have done your homework. Visit the school's website and read about their curriculum, mission statement, and values. Find out which communities and populations are served by the school. How do they describe their student body? Which extracurricular activities are available to students? Does the school promote research and innovation? Do you think the school's teaching methods will fit your learning style?

Being informed demonstrates your interest in the program, allowing you to highlight the following factors in your essays:

- How well you will fit in at the school, given your personal experiences, skills, attributes, and traits

- Common values and passions you share with the school or program

- Personal connections to the school or the community where the school is located (Do you have family, friends, or a support network nearby? Have you visited the area before?)

- Your specific interest in attending the school (Examples can include specific research interests, outreach to the community, and so forth)

Cultural competency

Questions about cultural competency or diversity delve into your ability to interact with people whose cultural traditions, beliefs, or values are different from your own. Are you able to help people in a way that is in line with their beliefs and values? Can you effectively communicate in a way that bridges cultural differences? Have you overcome any barriers that you faced with regards to cultural traditions or values, and how did you overcome them? What has helped you become a person that respects and values others' beliefs, as well as your own? You can highlight the following experiences in your essay:

- Advocating for others, especially those from different sociocultural or socioeconomic backgrounds

- Learning skills from people of different backgrounds

- Helping someone from a different background to solve a problem

- Communicating effectively with those from different backgrounds, overcoming language or cultural barriers

- Interacting with individuals whose values or opinions differ from your own

- Learning about and accepting the beliefs of people from different backgrounds

Overcoming challenges

This prompt is used to identify whether you possess traits such as resilience, discipline, and perseverance. Your professional life will inevitably present you with a variety of challenges, and schools are looking for candidates equipped with mature coping strategies that enable them to navigate these challenges effectively. Here are some ideas for experiences to highlight:

- A time when you failed or when something did not go according to plan

- How you overcame a setback

- Overcoming illness or injury, either in yourself or a loved one

- Overcoming significant personal or family hardships, such as a difficult upbringing, poor financial circumstances, or seeking asylum

- The strategies you used to overcome these challenges, what you learned from the experience, and how you will use these lessons in the future

When writing about overcoming challenges, it is important to stay positive and take responsibility for any setbacks and failures.

Career goals

This prompt is asking you to consider your future as a professional. To help generate some ideas, consider the following questions:

- What experiences have you had that solidified your decision to pursue a profession?

- What fascinates you the most about the profession, and why?

- Do you have an interest in a particular specialty in the profession? Why?

Academic lapses or breaks

If you have any academic lapses or breaks in your studies, this type of essay allows you to proactively explain what occurred and why. You may want to include the following:

- A brief explanation of the situation
- How you moved past the situation
- What you learned and what you would do if you encountered a similar situation in the future

Extracurricular activities

Programs want to know whether you are proactive and productive. You can demonstrate your commitment to your previous activities or highlight exciting new ventures.

- Have you kept up with your previous commitments, if possible?
- If you are taking a gap year, what are you doing and why?
- Are you productive with your time by volunteering, tutoring, and so forth?
- Are you also demonstrating work-life balance by engaging in hobbies?
- What are you planning on doing later in the year? What are your goals and why?

What else do you want us to know?

This catch-all prompt is often optional. Nevertheless, it is an opportunity to let Ivy League schools know more about you. It is strongly advised that you do not simply repeat something you have said in your other essays, if applicable, but rather offer something new. Here are some ideas:

- Discuss answers to questions that other schools asked but this one did not.

- Write about non-formal activities that informed your passion for a profession.

- Show that you are a well-rounded candidate by discussing other significant passions you may have.

- Provide any updates to your application.

- Further expand on what you have already noted previously.

How are essays evaluated by Ivy League schools?

Ivy League schools receive thousands of applications during each cycle. It is important to understand how your personal statement and supplemental essays will be evaluated. An easy way to remember how these essays will be evaluated is to think alliteratively: *quick, concise,* and *coherent*.

Quick:

Because of the volume of applications schools receive each year, reviewers will not be able to spend hours reviewing each essay. Rather, they must read them quickly, grasp your points, and form a judgment about your personality in a matter of minutes. An application essay is not the place to try fancy literary devices or unusual structures. **You must be clear and direct in your writing.**

On one hand, it may feel disheartening to think that the product of hours of work is going to be in the hands of reviewers for only a few fleeting minutes. On the other hand, you should feel comforted by the fact that your prose does not have to be complicated to impress an admissions committee.

Concise:

Your essays should succinctly answer the question (or questions) asked by the prompts, instantiating your points with examples. Use simple, direct, and clear language to show the reader your traits and skills through the personal experiences you have had. Make sure you are not merely telling the reader a set of facts.

Coherent:

To ensure that your essay is coherent, structure it in an academic format, with an introduction, two to four body paragraphs, and a conclusion. This straightforward organization will make your essay easy to navigate for the reader, enabling them to understand the points you are highlighting and quickly learn about your personality and traits. For some of the shorter essays, introductory or concluding paragraphs may not be necessary or possible, but they should still have a clear opening, a main point illustrated by examples, and an effective closing.

Who are the evaluators?

You may be wondering who exactly will be reading and evaluating your essays. Admissions committees may consist of a mix of directors or associate directors of admissions, admissions officers, deans, faculty members, or even current students. You do not need to name-drop or demonstrate the depth of your knowledge in your essay. Focus, instead, on explaining your reasons for pursuing a particular profession clearly and succinctly in a way that anyone can understand or relate to.

Just how important are these essays?

Every program has a unique way of evaluating essays. Some schools consider your application holistically and give it an overall score after considering all of its components, including the personal statement and supplemental essays, high school transcript or grades, college entrance exam test scores, activities, and letters of recommendation. Other programs will weight each component differently.

Can you overcome a low college entrance exam test score with a spectacular essay? Not exactly. You must ensure all aspects of your application are strong, including your personal statement and supplemental essays, high school transcript or grades, activities, and letters of recommendation. However, a strong essay can certainly push you from being an average applicant to a competitive one. Conversely, a weak personal statement with red flags can result in you not receiving an offer, despite your strong grades and college entrance exam test scores.

Essays, whether general or college-specific, lightly or heavily weighted, are an integral part of your application, and should be given the appropriate consideration when you are planning to apply to an Ivy League school. You should always seek to write the best essays possible.

CHAPTER II

Top 5 Reasons Applicants Get Rejected

Applying to an Ivy League school is a daunting, time-consuming, and expensive process. Before you begin to prepare your application, we want to give you an idea of the sorts of things that typically get an applicant rejected so you do not commit any of these errors. Your goal should be to apply with the strongest application possible, and hopefully let that be the only time you must go through the application cycle.

Below, you will find the top five mistakes you can make in your application and how they can impact your chances of moving forward.

1. Starting the application process too late

Application systems typically allow applicants to start submitting their applications in July or August of each year. This means your application, including your personal statement, should be completely ready to submit by this time. If you wait until the application system has opened to begin writing your personal statement, you risk rushing the writing process and settling for a weaker essay.

You must allow yourself time to brainstorm ideas, make an outline, draft your essay, receive honest feedback, and go through two to three revisions, possibly more, before you are happy with the result. A reasonable timeline for brainstorming, drafting, and revising your personal statement is approximately four to six weeks.

Of course, you may need to give yourself extra time based on your personal circumstances. If you are also occupied with work, studies, or family obligations, make sure you give yourself an extra two weeks of wiggle room to avoid falling behind.

A writing pearl to consider: Set aside time in your calendar for drafting your personal statement (as well as the rest of your application). Scheduling specific times to do this will make the process much more manageable and help you to stay focused without distraction.

2. Applying to unsuitable schools

When you are planning to apply to Ivy League schools, you may think it's best to cast your net as wide as possible. After all, isn't it better to apply to every Ivy League school to increase your chances of success?

The answer here is **no**. It would be counterproductive to apply to all the Ivy League schools, considering the time and effort required to apply to each one. Instead, you should narrow your focus to your top choices. This will allow you to concentrate your efforts. This will also reduce your workload when it comes to submitting essays.

How, though, will you begin to narrow down your list? There are two steps you must take to ensure that you are applying to suitable schools: 1) Research the schools you are interested in, and 2) ensure that your expectations are realistic.

First, take your time to research schools you are interested in. Individual school websites and repositories have a wealth of information available to you. In addition to statistics on the grades and college entrance exam test scores of students who were admitted in the previous cycle, you can also find the profile of the entering class, such as the number of in-state versus out-of-state students. Finally, you can read the school's mission statement and values and find out if they align with yours. Gather as much information as you can in this first step of selecting schools.

Next, you must ensure that the schools you apply to are ones you have a realistic and competitive chance of receiving acceptances from. Check that your grades and college entrance exam test scores are at, if not above, the medians or averages you found in your research. Carefully examine the class profiles to see whether you also have the kinds of experiences other successful applicants have had so you can ensure that you are the type of applicant the school is looking for. You should also reflect the values of the school through your personal experiences and highlight these experiences in your essays and activities.

You must be honest with yourself when selecting schools. There may be a program you have dreamed of attending or that is very prestigious, but if your grades and college entrance exam test scores are well below the median, this would not be a realistic school for you to apply to, and going forward with the application will only be a waste of your effort and lead to disappointment.

3. Including too many experiences in your essays

When you are forming an outline of your essay, you may feel tempted to include all the activities on your CV. You may have attended a major conference for one day or gave a speech at an event, so wouldn't it be helpful to mention these experiences in your essay?

No. A more effective plan would be for you to pick two to three impactful experiences through which to tell the readers your story. First, formulate a thesis statement that introduces the theme of your essay, such as why you have decided to pursue a profession. Then use the specific details in your two to three examples to *show* the reader how and why you decided to pursue the profession. Narrowing your essay's focus to a small number of experiences gives you the space to tell the story effectively and to show the values you embody. It will also ensure that your essay is cohesive, focused, and flows well. If you list too many activities, your essay will turn into a mere regurgitation of your CV or resume. Remember, you also have your activities section in Common App to highlight your other engagements.

There are two further points to consider when you are choosing which experiences to highlight: *commitment* and *progression*.

- *Commitment:* The best experiences to highlight are the ones that you have participated in regularly for a long time. Rather than including experiences that you engaged in briefly for one day or a few weeks, choose those that you have engaged in consistently over a period of several months, or preferably, years. Highlighting a long-term commitment shows your dedication to that activity, even when you are busy with other things, such as exams.

  Pick these: volunteering at a shelter every week for the last year, playing basketball from high school through university, being a member of a band that has performed regularly for the last three years

  Not these: attending a conference for one day, giving a speech at an event, participating in a project for two months

- *Progression:* Reflect on your experiences and highlight ones in which you made progress, your role evolved, or your responsibilities increased. You want to showcase your capacity to learn and grow, so it is best to choose activities where you have been able to advance and transform in your role through time. This will also highlight your ability to take initiative and step up to leadership positions.

  Pick these: starting as a committee member in a school group and becoming a vice-president, being the captain of your intramural team, leading a project that involved supervising others

  Not these: participating in the same volunteer role over the course of several years, working in a paid position in which you have not yet been promoted

Commitment and progression are important to consider, but there are also effective ways to include activities that do not show either. For example, you may discuss your one-day conference attendance as a part of the general activity that you have been engaged in for a long time.

4. Missing the point of the questions asked

Although it may seem surprising, a common reason for not having a successful Ivy League application is simply that the applicant did not answer the questions asked by the prompts. It often results from students getting fixated on including as many experiences and skills as they can, thereby missing the point of the question.

If you do not answer the actual question that was posed, the reader will think you lack attention to detail or that you were merely using the essay as an opportunity to put your achievements on display. They will get no sense of your prospect as a student, or as a future professional, and will likely think you cannot self-reflect. All these judgments will reflect poorly on you and result in your application being passed over.

For all essay prompts, make sure you have read the prompt carefully. If the school has asked you to demonstrate your cultural competency, you need to reflect on your experiences and include only those that are relevant to this skill. Merely using the essay as an opportunity to discuss your achievements will result in you missing the purpose of this question. Additionally, if a prompt has multiple questions, be sure to address all the questions throughout your essay.

5. Poorly written essays or entries

Once you have chosen the right schools to apply to, picked appropriate activities to discuss, and started drafting your essay, you will probably think the hard work is over. After all, you have an outline and your work is almost done, right?

Well, no, because you must now ensure that your essay is written well. Poorly written essays are difficult to follow, and the points you are attempting to make will not come across to the readers. Sloppy writing is the top reason why your personal statement will be received poorly by the admissions committee, and your efforts will have been wasted.

To write an effective essay, you must first structure it in an academic format with an introduction, body paragraphs, and a conclusion. This will ensure your essay flows well, making it easy for the reader to follow your story from one point to the next.

Second, make sure you are *showing* and not merely *telling*. You cannot simply list off qualities and skills you possess and expect the reader to believe you. Rather, you must demonstrate these qualities through specific examples from your experiences. For instance, instead of just saying "I am a good communicator," you can share an anecdote about a time you used good communication skills to accomplish a goal: "We were working on a group project when two of my teammates got into a conflict over the next step to take. To resolve the conflict, I had a private conversation with each individual to understand their points of view. I then suggested we incorporate suggestions from each team member to move forward." This example goes beyond listing your communication, leadership, and collaboration skills by illustrating how you used them to solve a problem.

Third, describe your experiences using simple, direct language. You do not want the reviewers puzzling over what they just read. Rather, you want your points to be immediately clear, given how quickly the committee will be reading your essays.

Fourth, read through your final draft carefully multiple times to ensure that there are no grammatical errors, misspellings, or typos. This point often seems minor to students, but any errors in your writing will reflect negatively on you. Professionals must communicate effectively through written documents, so you must demonstrate that you are capable of this through your essays. Having an error-free essay shows the reader you are meticulous and detail-oriented in your work, and that you are a mature individual who can communicate like a professional.

Now that you have become aware of some common 'faux pas' when approaching applications, we can begin focusing on the personal statement. In the next chapter, we will specifically discuss the common errors that applicants make while writing their essays. Let's take a closer look!

CHAPTER III

7 Common Essay Errors

In the previous chapter, we discussed common reasons for applicants to get rejected. The last reason we explored was poorly written essays. Now, an essay can be weak for many reasons. Based on our experiences, our experts have compiled a list of common errors found in poorly written essays. In this chapter, we will take a closer look at these errors and how you can avoid making the same mistakes.

This is very important, so take notes. Are you ready? Let's go!

1. Poor grammar and spelling

The #1 common error we find in essays is poor grammar and spelling. These may seem like obvious errors to avoid, yet every year, students submit essays with grammatical, punctuation, or spelling mistakes because they are rushed and do not leave themselves with enough time to thoroughly read through their final drafts.

Consequently, students present themselves as sloppy and lacking attention to detail. That is not something we want the admissions committee to think of you!

Remember, professionals must write clearly and effectively, so you need to communicate in an error-free manner. You can start communicating like a professional right now by eliminating any errors from your essays.

Do not rely solely on your computer's word processing software to catch grammatical errors as they are not failsafe. When you have finished writing your essay, leave time to thoroughly read a printed hard copy from start to finish, multiple times, with a critical eye. You can also read your essay out loud to yourself, as this will often help you to catch errors you would otherwise miss by simply scanning the document.

2. Using clichés or informal language

"To be, or not to be? That is the question." Using a cliché phrase is as ineffective as quoting the most referenced line from William Shakespeare. Because we have heard it many times before, using such phrases adds nothing to the creativity and originality of your essay, which can actually do more harm than good.

Applicants tend to use clichés when describing what aspirations they have and why. For example, many students want to enter a profession so they can "help people" or "serve others." Although these may be genuine reasons, they are overused phrases in application essays. Having these phrases in your essays will lead the admissions committee to think that you have not thought deeply enough about your intrinsic motivations or gained enough experience or knowledge to enter the profession.

Rather than saying you want to "help people" or "serve others," dig deeper into the specific reasons why you wish to study a particular field. There are many professions in which you can help others. What is it about this field specifically that has drawn you in? What experiences did you seek that are related to the field, and how did they impact your decision? What did you learn about yourself from these experiences, and how do you think you will apply this in your profession? It is a 'personal' essay, in every sense of the word. It's about you and your unique story!

Sometimes, when we are speaking about ourselves, we naturally lapse into casual language, peppering our stories with "like," using short forms such as "undergrad," and referring to institutions or programs using acronyms only we recognize. However, informal language like this will make your essay seem too casual and give the reviewer the impression that you did not spend enough time or effort writing it. You must remember that your essay, though about you, is still a formal document that must be written in a professional way. You want admissions committees to know you are approaching the application process seriously, and with thoughtfulness and maturity.

3. Listing your experiences like a CV or resume

Your essay is going to be a tempting place to list every single one of your experiences! You may find it difficult to exclude any of the great volunteering positions you've held, the extracurricular activities you're engaged in, and the research experiences you've had. However, there are at least two reasons for avoiding this approach.

First, there are already designated places, such as in your CV, for you to list your experiences and achievements. Common App has an activities section in which you have space to list the many activities you have participated in that may or may not be highlighted in your essay. Using your personal statement to list all these activities again would therefore be redundant.

More importantly, recall that your essay should be used to *show* your skills, abilities, and knowledge. If you list every item on your CV, you will only be able to *tell* the reader what you have done, without expanding on any one experience. It is better to pick a smaller number of experiences, between two and three, and take the time to expand on each one in more detail. You need space to describe each experience, give specific details or examples of interactions, and reflect on why that experience was significant in your journey to pursuing your field of study.

4. Poor structure and flow

As we mentioned earlier, readers review your personal statement quickly. It is therefore important that your essay is easy to read and follow.

Students tend to structure the first drafts of their essays poorly. There is often no thesis statement or theme to make the essay cohesive, and paragraphs and ideas are not always linked together with logical transitions. If your essay is structured in this manner, it will be difficult for readers to follow your thoughts and pick out your ideas because they will be too distracted by their attempt to find the threads of your essay! You must craft an essay that anyone can understand easily, one in which your key points are front and center, and your narrative is what the reader remembers.

Have a strong thesis statement that emerges in your first paragraph and reinforce it in all subsequent paragraphs. Each section of your essay should be linked with strong transitional statements and phrases that make clear connections between your ideas. Instead of hopping back and forth in time, try orienting the reader by following a chronological order when you are describing your experiences. Your conclusion should include a summary of the thoughts you have introduced in your essay, as well as a callback to the theme you introduced in the opening paragraph.

A poorly structured essay that does not flow well will frustrate the reader and hurt your application. A strongly structured one, on the other hand, will make your thoughts easy to follow and your points accessible, allowing the reader to learn more about you.

5. Red flags

At all stages of the application process, the admissions committee is looking for 'red flags.' These are any indicators showing that you are unprofessional, lacking in maturity, dishonest, or insincere in your application. Red flags may also indicate that you are a poor communicator or unable to cope with challenging situations. Readers who have evaluated hundreds of essays can quickly identify these, making it easy for the committee to rule you out. Even though you write the personal statement yourself, it can still contain red flags. You must be careful to always come across as a mature, thoughtful professional.

The following are some common red flags reviewers might identify:

- DISHONESTY: Dishonesty is taken very seriously and will result in an automatic disqualification of your application from consideration. Do not exaggerate, make up, or embellish any of your experiences. The application asks for letters of recommendation for a reason, and these types of falsehoods are easy to check. Not only is dishonesty unethical, but it is also not worth the risk.

- UNPROFESSIONAL BEHAVIOR: You need to submit your documents on time and in a completed state. Not doing so shows unprofessional behavior and reflects poorly on your prospect as a professional. All interactions described in your essays should be discussed respectfully and with care to protect the confidentiality of any individuals involved, especially vulnerable parties.

- POOR COMMUNICATION SKILLS: Even though you may think essays reveal only your writing skills, the admissions committee will flag you as a poor communicator if you submit a crudely written essay. Since both verbal and written communication are important for a professional's day-to-day role, any indication of poor writing skills will disqualify you from moving forward in the application process.

- INABILITY TO COPE WITH CHALLENGES: You may have faced failures and challenges in your journey. This is okay, and we will dedicate some time later to discuss how to address academic discrepancies in your essay. For now, keep in mind that you must address any challenges proactively, focusing on your involvement and responsibilities, refraining from blaming others, and discussing what you learned and how this learning will influence your future behavior. You must show that you are able to handle difficult situations and resolve conflicts, since you will inevitably face many such situations as a professional.

6. No expert feedback

Most students find essay writing to be daunting, and inevitably seek guidance from their family members or friends. However, it can be difficult to know who to ask for help. Should you ask your best friend? The classmate who excels in English? A first-year Ivy League student? The neighbor in graduate school because she writes a lot?

We recommend that you get feedback from an expert. This is someone who not only has knowledge of the admissions process and a sense of what makes for a strong personal statement, but also has extensive experience reviewing essays like yours. Their past experience with other students' essays will allow them to pick out any common mistakes you might be making and guide you on how to fix them. An expert will be able to read your first draft, give you suggestions for improvements, read subsequent drafts, and continue to give you recommendations until your personal statement is as strong as it can be.

Another reason we recommend seeking expert feedback, as opposed to asking friends or family, is that an expert is objective. Your family members and friends, being close to you, are going to try to see the best in whatever you do and can be hesitant to provide critical feedback, especially if you are writing about your personal experiences. Naturally, they do not want to hurt your feelings and may not be able to objectively identify the parts of your essay that need work. An expert who does not know you personally can bring objectivity to the process. They can comment on any parts of your essay without regard for which experiences you are writing about. This person will be able to focus on whether you are effectively describing why you want to study a particular field and how you have reached that decision, as well as give you the critical, honest feedback that you need to improve your essay.

7. Too many cooks in the kitchen

Since feedback is so useful for shaping and refining your personal statement, shouldn't you seek feedback from multiple people? Aren't two heads better than one?

Actually, when it comes to writing a personal statement, too many heads can be worse than one! Sometimes, an expert will be giving you feedback, while family members and friends begin contradicting the expert or suggesting that you make additional changes. This will inevitably lead to confusion for you, the applicant. We refer to this as having 'too many cooks in the kitchen.'

The metaphor is straightforward. Imagine there are too many chefs crammed into a kitchen, all trying to teach you how to cook the same dish. One adds spices, while another stirs. A third is reciting the recipe, and a fourth is turning up the heat. One thinks there is enough salt, while another wants you to add more. They are all barking out conflicting instructions, but no one is listening to anyone else. The dish is heading toward disaster. What do you do?

Now, imagine being taught to make that same dish by an expert chef who works one-to-one with you. The expert guides you step-by-step through the process, giving you meticulous directions so that you not only end up making a great-tasting dish, but you also learn important cooking skills along the way. You are only working with one person, so you are never confused about directions. You have a great time, and the product is both aesthetically pleasing and delicious!

The same principle applies to writing essays. If you seek feedback from multiple sources, those people can begin to contradict each other. You may get confused and wonder whose directions to follow. We hope you do not find yourself in this situation. If you do, our advice is to work only with an expert, and not complicate the process by involving family members and friends who, as discussed previously, can be subjective. Receiving feedback from one expert source throughout your essay revising process will ensure that you receive well-grounded and consistent feedback. Following the expert's guidance and advice will allow you to steadily improve your essay. When you are finished, you can be certain that you have the best possible version of your personal statement for submission.

Hopefully, you now have a better understanding of what common errors to avoid when approaching your personal statement. In the next chapter, we will look at sample personal statements from past BeMo students. There, you will have the opportunity to pinpoint some of the errors we just discussed, and we will give you a glimpse of the expert feedback process from beginning to end. In observing the full process, we hope that you will have more confidence approaching your own essay.

Free goodwill

A message from our CEO, Behrouz Moemeni

My mentor always used to say, "Behrouz, you should give until it hurts." What he meant by this is giving your time and resources to those who are less fortunate or experienced than you to empower them to get to the next level on their journey, whatever that may be. People who lend a hand to others with zero expectations for return experience higher life satisfaction and self-fulfillment and are generally more successful in their careers. However, I have learned that supporting others can be a lot simpler than what you may think. You don't have to spend a lot of time or money, and it doesn't actually have to "hurt" to help. It starts with the simple things and grows as you gain the resources to do more.

As you probably know, I created BeMo to provide as much information as possible to everyone. I think information should be available to all for little to no cost. That's why, at BeMo, we create books, videos, extensive blogs, and other resources at little to no cost to students, even though they cost us a lot to create. We only charge for our private consulting and preparation programs, and even then, the value we create for our students is infinitely more than the cost of our services. For example, think of the lifetime value of becoming a medical doctor, dentist, lawyer, business leader, and so forth (e.g., by doing some quick math and multiplying only 20 years of work at an average of $250,000/year salary). Though the return on investment is crystal clear, we want students to start with a low-cost commitment to see the benefit first; we want students to choose us to be their private mentors only if they find value in our work and commit only when they are ready to invest in themselves, which we facilitate with interest-free installment plans. This is why we provide all the information necessary for anyone to do this on their own, if they choose to do so. However, the only way for us, at BeMo, to accomplish our audacious mission of helping one billion students is by reaching as many people as possible.

So, I'd like to create an opportunity for you to help others you don't know with a few minutes of your time. Think of those who will go through the same journey as you in the future. They are less experienced, have less resources, and maybe have no idea where to start. If you have found the information in this book valuable so far, would you please write us a quick review on Amazon?

Most people judge a book like this by its cover and its reviews. Your review will help someone ...

get to the next level ...

advance in their career ...

achieve life fulfillment ...

and ... *help others*.

It will take you less than 60 seconds to make all of this happen ... please leave a review on Amazon.

Thank you very much from the bottom of my heart for helping us with our mission.

To your success,
Behrouz Moemeni, Ph.D.
CEO @ BeMo

CHAPTER IV

10 Personal Statement Examples: From First Draft to Acceptance-Magnet Final Draft

Now that you understand the common errors in a personal statement, let's put your knowledge to the test. In this chapter, we will go through 10 personal statements from past BeMo students and show you the feedback process from beginning to end. For all personal statements, we removed personal identifiers to protect the students' confidentiality.

For each personal statement, we will first show the essay in its raw form when it was initially sent in for review. After you have read the unrevised first draft, you will have an opportunity to identify the common errors outlined in *Chapter III: 7 Common Essay Errors*. We will then highlight the errors one of our admissions experts identified and discuss the specific ways in which each personal statement can be improved. Next, we will show you the first revision made by the expert, which will contain corrections and comments throughout. Lastly, you will get to see the final draft of the personal statement after the student has made revisions using our feedback. Note that in most cases, it takes more than one revision to arrive at the final product. However, since the purpose of this exercise is to demonstrate the progression of the essay and the impact of expert feedback, we will only show you the first draft and the final draft. The actual number of revisions can vary based on the quality of the initial essay submitted, the number of changes required, and the student's willingness and ability to integrate our comments and suggestions.

As we go through each stage of improving these personal statements, take notes and refer to the previous chapters as needed to work through the exercise. Note that the sample essays are based on Common App, which has a limit of 650 words for these essays.

To break it down again, you will see the following for each sample essay:

a. First draft: The exact copy sent in by a student for a BeMo review.

b. Exercise: Your opportunity to list the errors you find throughout the essay. Pay close attention to not only grammatical errors, but also to structural and organizational issues.

c. List of errors: A list of errors our admissions expert has identified and explanations of what the student should and should not do.

d. First revision by an expert: The first review by one of our admissions experts, including revisions and comments.

e. Final draft: The final draft after the student has considered our feedback and made revisions based on our suggestions.

f. Discussion: An overview of the changes that were made and a discussion of how the applicant was able to alter their personal statement to completely transform it into an acceptance magnet!

Are you ready? Here we go!

The personal statement prompt: Consider a time when you disagreed with the ideas or beliefs of someone else. How did you reconcile these differing perspectives?

1a. First draft

Families want the best for each other, but that does not necessarily mean that they always agree. I often ask my family members for advice because I respect them and want to know their perspective. Of course, I wanted my family's advice when I was thinking about my future career. My family encouraged me to study something practical that would lead to a stable job. This appealed to me, but I also wanted to have a job that I enjoyed doing every day.

I always loved art history. I could spend hours wandering around the museum and reading the placards for each piece. During long afternoons spent at the museum, I felt like I was stepping back in time and seeing how other people lived, worked, and created. Each piece of art told a story about the artist and their community, the things they loved, their hopes and fears, and how they saw the world. I wanted to be an observer but also an expert. However, I knew that my family would disagree with any decision to pursue a liberal arts degree simply because jobs are not as prevalent as they would be for other degrees.

Every good decision requires research, so I set out to learn more about art history programs, careers, and opportunities. When choosing a career, it is not enough to just have an interest. You also need to understand how a degree translates into an income that will meet at least your basic needs and expectations. Quality of life is a product of both financial independence and the intrinsic happiness achieved through pursuing something you love. Consequently, I was thrilled to discover that an art history degree is the basis for a wide variety of careers. An obvious career path would involve becoming a gallery or museum manager, but there were many other options available. I could become an auction specialist, curator, teacher, professor, librarian, author, archivist, or art therapy practitioner, among other possibilities.

Besides a love for art history, I also had a strong drive to teach others. My research led me to realize that an art history degree did not have to mean a career limited to an art gallery or museum job. I could become a scholar, which would allow me to research my passion, as well as share it with the next generation of students. Further, this career would give me the flexibility and opportunity to pursue positions in a diverse range of schools at home and abroad. This career would open up the world to me rather than restricting me.

31

I came to realize that my family's opposition to a liberal arts education was a gift. It gave me the motivation to do research and make an argument for why a liberal arts program would be the best option for me. It also required me to consider the financial implications of different job opportunities for people with a liberal arts background. I reflected on what would be acceptable to me and what sacrifices I was willing to make to work in a job that I found to be personally satisfying.

When disagreeing with others, especially family members, it's easy to assume that they will stay staunch in their opinions. I was surprised to find that once I presented my family with my research, they were very supportive of me. My research demonstrated to them that art history was important to me, and it also gave them an appreciation for opportunities available through a liberal arts degree that they were not aware of.

I truly believe that differences in opinions are an opportunity to grow. My family's strong opinions against a humanities education motivated me to ask critical questions that I might not have considered otherwise. Working through these questions renewed my confidence in what my instincts were telling me, which was that this was the correct path for me. In the end, I am pursuing an art history degree because I was placed in a position to question it's practicality and relevance to my situation.

1b. Exercise: Can you spot the errors?

Use the space below to write down the errors you have spotted. Make sure you do this before moving on to the next section. Besides identifying grammatical errors, also make note of red flags, issues with structure and flow, and so forth. Take your time and refer to *Chapter III: 7 Common Essay Errors* if necessary.

1c. List of errors

Now let's examine the errors our admissions expert identified. To help you better understand our approach, these errors will be bolded and underlined in the revised draft in the following section.

- *Not concise:* The applicant can make their writing more concise by replacing or removing unnecessary and repetitive words and phrases.

- *Minor punctuation errors:* The essay contains minor punctuation errors that will be distracting to the reader. These can be easily identified through a detailed review of the entire essay.

- *Ineffective transitions:* Transitions between sentences and paragraphs can be improved.

- *Weak conclusion:* The conclusion should be expanded and end on a memorable note as it is the admission committee's last impression of the applicant.

- *Too long:* This essay exceeds the upper limit for Common App submissions, which is 650 words. The essay needs to be condensed to fall below that upper limit.

Note: The passages in which the expert left comments or suggestions for the student to review are underlined and marked using superscript numerals. Use these numerals to reference our expert's comments/suggestions listed below the revised draft.

1d. First revision by a BeMo admissions expert

Families want the best for each other, but that does not ~~necessarily~~[1] mean that they always agree. I often ask ~~my~~[2] family members for advice because I respect them and want to know their ~~perspective~~ **perspectives**.[3] Of course, I wanted my family's advice when I was thinking about my future ~~career~~ **profession**.[4] My family encouraged me to study something practical that would lead to a stable job. ~~This~~ **Stability**[5] appealed to me, but I also wanted to have a job that I enjoyed doing every day.

I always loved art history. I could spend hours wandering around the museum and reading the placards for each piece. During long afternoons spent at the museum, I felt like I was stepping back in time and seeing how other people lived, worked, and created. Each ~~piece of art~~ **art piece**[6] told a story about the artist and their community, the things they loved, their hopes and fears, and how they saw the world. **I wanted to be an observer but also an expert.**[7] However, I knew that my family would disagree with any decision to pursue a liberal arts degree simply because ~~jobs are not as prevalent as they would be for other degrees~~ **there are limited jobs available**.[8]

Every good decision requires research, so I set out to learn more about art history programs~~, careers,~~[9] and opportunities. When choosing a ~~career~~ **profession**,[10] it is not enough to ~~just~~[11] have an interest. You also need to understand how a degree translates into an income that will meet ~~at least~~[12] your basic needs and expectations. Quality of life is a product of ~~both~~[13] financial independence and the intrinsic happiness achieved through pursuing something you ~~love~~ **enjoy**.[14] Consequently, I was thrilled to discover that an art history degree is the basis for a wide variety of careers. An obvious ~~career path~~ **choice**[15] would involve becoming a gallery or museum manager, but there were many other options available. I could become an auction specialist, curator, teacher, professor, librarian, author, archivist, or art therapy practitioner, among other possibilities.

Besides ~~a love~~ **my passion**[16] for art history, I also had a strong drive to teach others. ~~My research led me to realize that an~~ **An**[17] art history degree did not have to mean a career limited to an art gallery or museum job. ~~I could become a scholar, which would allow me to research my passion~~ **As a professor and scholar, I could develop my expertise in art history,**[18] as well as share it with the next generation of students. Further, this career would give me the flexibility and opportunity to pursue positions in a diverse range of schools at home and abroad. ~~This career would open up the world to me rather than restricting me.~~[19]

I came to realize that my family's opposition to a liberal arts education was a gift.[20] It gave me the motivation to ~~do~~ **perform**[21] research and make an argument for why a liberal arts program would be the best option for me. It also required me to consider the financial implications of different job opportunities for people with a liberal arts background. I reflected on what would be acceptable to me and what sacrifices I was willing to make to work in a job that I found to be personally satisfying.

When disagreeing with others, especially family members, it's easy to assume that they will stay staunch in their opinions. I was surprised to find that once I presented my family with my research, they were very supportive of me. My research demonstrated to them that art history was important to me, and it also gave them an appreciation for opportunities available through a liberal arts degree ~~that they were not aware of~~.[22]

~~I truly believe that~~ **Differences**[23] in opinions are an opportunity to grow. My family's strong opinions against a liberal arts education motivated me to ask critical questions that I might not have considered otherwise. Working through these questions renewed my confidence in what my instincts were telling me, which was that this was the correct path for me. **In the end, I am pursuing an art history degree because I was placed in a position to question ~~it's~~ its**[24] **practicality and relevance to my situation.**[25]

Word count prior to revision: 675

Word count after revision: 628

Word count limit: 650

Expert's comments/suggestions:

1. You've exceeded the upper word count limit for a Common App essay. Look for opportunities to remove unnecessary words or phrases. For example, the word "necessarily" can be removed from this statement without changing your meaning.

2. You don't need to include "my" as it's implied by your other content.

3. This statement discusses "family members" (plural), so "perspectives" should also be plural.

4. A more accurate word to use is "profession," which refers to your area of expertise. "Career" refers to a specific job.

5. Be careful when using the word "This" as your meaning could be vague. Replace it with a specific word, in this case, "Stability."

6. Reduce your phrasing to improve conciseness. Your essay will be easier to read, and you will also expand your available word count.

7. This sentence seems out of place. Create a stronger transition between this sentence and the sentences that come before and after.

8. This phrasing can be reduced to make your essay more concise and increase your available word count.

9. Your space is limited. It's sufficient to simply refer to "opportunities," which encompasses possible careers.

10. As mentioned in an earlier comment, "profession" is a preferable word to use.

11. Remove unnecessary words that don't add value to your content or that aren't required for grammatical reasons.

12. These words are unnecessary to convey your meaning and can be removed for conciseness.

13. This word can be removed as it increases your word count and does not enhance clarity.

14. This word is used frequently throughout your essay. For variety, take the time to identify words that are repeated often in your essay and replace them.

15. Look for opportunities to make your wording more concise.

16. Replace any words that are used frequently in your essay. Besides adding variety, you will avoid distracting the reader with repetitive wording.

17. This phrase can be removed to increase your available word count. It's not crucial to your meaning.

18. The original phrase was repetitive and lacked specificity. Focus on the concept of developing expertise.

19. This sentence doesn't provide information to support your essay and can be removed.

20. This new paragraph starts abruptly and would benefit from a better transition.

21. This wording is somewhat casual. There are better alternatives, such as "perform."

22. This phrase does not add any value to the sentence. Removing it will also increase your available word count.

23. This phrase can be updated to remove unnecessary words.

24. Punctuation errors, like this one, can be identified and corrected by taking the time to review your essay in detail before finalizing it.

25. Your conclusion, and particularly your concluding sentence, is your last opportunity to make an impression on the admissions committee. Spend some time to make this sentence unique and memorable so that your essay stands out from those of other applicants.

Our expert's overall feedback in the end:

Congratulations on completing your first draft! I enjoyed reading your response to the essay prompt.

Your introductory sentence is engaging and encourages the reader's interest. The subject of your essay will resonate with many readers who have also struggled with balancing their personal desires against family expectations. However, your conclusion is not as engaging. Spend some time to make your ending unique and memorable.

Your essay can be improved by removing or replacing unnecessary or repetitive words and phrases. These changes have two benefits: your essay will be easier to read, and you will increase your available word count. Additionally, as this is a formal essay, ensure that your remaining wording is appropriate and accurate.

Your biggest challenge in subsequent drafts will be reducing your word count. The Common App system used by all eight Ivy League schools has a strict word count range of 250 to 650 words. The system will not accept essay submissions outside of these limits. Your first draft exceeds the upper limit and will need to be reduced, which can be accomplished by incorporating the recommended changes.

Your essay revisions may change your word count. Ensure that your word count adheres to the limits defined for this essay prompt.

Please work on the areas outlined above and submit another draft for review when you're ready!

Cheers,
BeMo

The following document is a final draft that was the result of multiple revisions with our admissions expert. Typically, there are two to three revisions.

1e. Final draft

Families want the best for each other, but that does not mean they always agree. I often ask family members for advice because I respect them and want to know their perspectives. Of course, I wanted my family's advice when considering my future profession. My family encouraged me to study something practical that would lead to a stable job. Stability appealed to me, but I also wanted to have a job that I enjoyed.

I always loved art history. I could spend hours wandering around the museum and reading the placards for each piece. During long afternoons spent at the museum, I felt like I was stepping back in time and observing how other people lived, worked, and created. Each art piece told a story about the artist and their community, the things they treasured, their hopes and fears, and how they saw the world. I could envision a future career related to art history, but my family disagreed with this pursuit simply because there are limited jobs available.

Every good decision requires supporting evidence, so I researched art history opportunities. When choosing a profession, it is not enough to have an interest. You also need to understand how a degree translates into an income that will meet your basic needs. Quality of life is a product of financial independence and the intrinsic happiness achieved through pursuing something you enjoy. Consequently, I was thrilled to discover that an art history degree is the basis for a wide variety of careers, including auction specialist, curator, teacher, professor, librarian, author, archivist, and art therapy practitioner, among other possibilities.

Besides my passion for art history, I also had a strong drive to teach others. An art history degree did not have to mean a career limited to an art gallery or museum job. As a professor and scholar, I could develop my expertise in art history, as well as share it with the next generation of students. Further, this career would give me the flexibility to pursue positions in a diverse range of educational institutes at home and abroad.

My family's opposition to a liberal arts education gave me the motivation to perform research and make a case for why an art history degree would be the best option for me. It also required me to consider the financial implications of different job opportunities for people with this background. I reflected on what was acceptable to me and what sacrifices I was willing to make to work in a job that I found to be personally satisfying. Working through these questions renewed my confidence in what my instincts were telling me, which was that art history was the correct path for me. I was surprised to find that once I presented my family with my research, they were very supportive of my decision. My research demonstrated to them that art history was important to me, and it also gave them an appreciation for opportunities available through a liberal arts education. As I discovered, differences in opinions are a gift and an opportunity to grow into ourselves with confidence.

1f. Discussion

The applicant's first essay draft provided a good foundation for subsequent drafts, but it was much too long. It exceeded the word count limit for the application system and would have been rejected at its original length. The final draft is significantly shorter and falls within the accepted word count range. Besides applying the recommended changes from the expert review, the applicant also made their writing more concise overall, focusing specifically on content that would support their message.

The final draft no longer has minor punctuation errors or poor wording choices that are distracting to readers. Transitions between sentences and paragraphs have also been approved to guide the reader from one idea to the next.

The applicant's original conclusion was not unique or memorable. The new conclusion is substantially longer and ends on a positive note that will leave a lasting impression on the reader.

The personal statement prompt: Describe a situation when you had to make a choice that challenged a personal value. What did you learn from this experience?

2a. First draft

Speaking out against one of my colleagues was one of the most difficult decisions I've ever had to make, not only because it would damage our working relationship, but also because I was an intern student. By revealing an incident with a senior colleague, I might put my internship at risk, as well as my professional reputation. In effect, I would be damaging my career before it even started. One of my tasks as an intern was to do a final review of external training documents before sending them for printing, which included light editing and formatting. While reviewing the chapters prepared by my colleague, I noticed something amiss. The writing style and tone was very different from earlier chapters this colleague submitted. When I uploaded the new chapters to our copyright tool, it became clear that much of the content had been taken directly from another source. If I submitted the document for publishing, I would be complicit in copyright infringement, which would put my organization at legal risk. Although I knew that sharing this information with my manager could have personal, academic, and professional consequences for me, I had to do what was right. I informed my manager of what I had discovered, and my colleague was required to re-do the work. My manager assured me that I took the correct action. However, my relationship with my colleague was strained after that rather than friendly. It was a small sacrifice to make to uphold my values.

2b. Exercise: Can you spot the errors?

Use the space below to write down the errors you have spotted. Make sure you do this before moving on to the next section. Besides identifying grammatical errors, also make note of red flags, issues with structure and flow, and so forth. Take your time and refer to *Chapter III: 7 Common Essay Errors* if necessary.

2c. List of errors

Now let's examine the errors our admissions expert identified. To help you better understand our approach, these errors will be bolded and underlined in the revised draft in the following section.

- *Weak introduction:* While the content of the introductory sentence is compelling, the way it is presented is not. Starting the essay with a question, quote, or description of a significant moment will capture the reader's attention.

- *Poor organization and structure:* The essay is difficult to follow because it is not in chronological order. Additionally, the applicant did not organize the essay into paragraphs, which will challenge the reader to identify the distinct ideas presented.

- *Poor word choice and phrasing:* The applicant occasionally uses casual language or awkward phrasing, which is distracting to the reader. The tone of the essay should be polished and professional.

- *Not concise:* The applicant has opportunities to improve the conciseness of the essay by replacing or removing unnecessary words and phrases.

- *Weak conclusion:* The conclusion summarizes the main points from the essay but does not connect back to the idea of honesty. It is crucial to make a final statement about honesty in the conclusion as this concept is central to the essay prompt.

- *Too short:* The Common App system used by all eight Ivy League schools has a word count range of 250 to 650 words. The system will not accept essays with word counts below or above these amounts. This essay is below 250 words.

Note: The passages in which the expert left comments or suggestions for the student to review are underlined and marked using superscript numerals. Use these numerals to reference our expert's comments/suggestions listed below the revised draft.

2d. First revision by a BeMo admissions expert

<u>Speaking out against one of my colleagues was one of the most difficult decisions I've ever made</u> ~~had to make~~,[1] <u>not only because it would damage our working relationship, but also because I was an intern student.</u>[2] By revealing an incident with a senior colleague, I <u>risked my internship</u> ~~might put my internship at risk~~,[3] as well as my professional reputation. ~~In effect,~~[4] I would be damaging my career before it even started.

    <u>One of my tasks as an intern was to perform</u> ~~do~~[5] <u>a final review of external training documents before sending them for printing, which included light editing and formatting.</u>[6] While reviewing the chapters prepared by my colleague, I noticed something amiss. The writing style and tone was very different from earlier chapters this colleague submitted. **<u>When I uploaded the new chapters to our copyright tool, it became clear that much of the content had been taken directly from another source.</u>**[7] If I submitted the document for publishing, I would be complicit in copyright infringement, which would put my organization at legal risk. Although I knew that sharing this information with my manager could have personal, academic, and professional consequences for me, I had to **do what was right.**[8] I informed my manager of what I had discovered, and my colleague was required to re-do the work.

    <u>My manager assured me that I took the correct action.</u>[9] However, my relationship with my colleague was **strained after that rather than friendly.**[10] It was a small sacrifice to make to uphold **my values.**[11]

Word count prior to revision: 248

Word count after revision: 241

Word count limit: 650

Expert's comments/suggestions:

1. Be concise. Your essay needs to be easy to read, allowing the admissions committee to grasp your key points quickly.

2. The content of your introductory sentence might capture the reader's attention, but your sentence structure and approach is not creative. To make your introduction more compelling, consider starting with a question, quote, or description of a significant moment related to your story.

3. This phrase could be more concise. You can condense this phrase, as shown, without changing your meaning.

4. This phrase is unnecessary and doesn't lend any value to your statement. I recommend removing it for conciseness.

5. Ensure that you are using the best words to capture your meaning. Use precise words instead of generic words.

6. As shown, this sentence is a good place to start a new paragraph as the topic changes. However, be sure to transition from the previous paragraph.

7. Some readers may not be familiar with copyright tools or their function. Expand on this statement to clarify the purpose of this tool.

8. Avoid using informal language in a formal essay. Your language should be polished and professional.

9. As shown, a new paragraph should start here as you are discussing a new idea.

10. This wording is awkward and would benefit from being rewritten.

11. Be sure to specifically refer to honesty when closing your essay given that it's the subject of the essay prompt.

Our expert's overall feedback in the end:

Thank you for sharing this difficult experience. Values such as honesty are often taken for granted until we encounter an ethical dilemma that challenges them. In your case, you had to choose between your value of honesty and maintaining a cordial working relationship with a colleague who violated this value.

Your essay starts by presenting the dilemma you faced, which is how many other applicants will answer this prompt. Differentiate yourself by using a creative opening, such as a question, quote, or description of a significant moment in your story.

The overall organization and structure of your essay would benefit from revision. The essay seems out of order. Before discussing the outcome of your internal conflict (that is, speaking out against your colleague), describe what led to that event. The reader will be able to follow the story more easily if it's in chronological order. Also, assist the reader in identifying the individual ideas in your story by organizing the essay into distinct paragraphs.

As you complete your final draft, replace or remove unnecessary words and phrases. You can use this additional space to expand on your key points, which should place a targeted focus on the essay prompt.

In your concluding paragraph, objectively summarize your essay while returning to the concept of honesty. The essay prompt specifically refers to the value of honesty. Therefore, it should be addressed in your closing.

Remember that the Common App system used by all eight Ivy League schools has a minimum word count of 250 words. The system will not accept essays below this word count. Currently, your word count is below 250 words, so you will need to expand on your discussion.

Your essay revisions may change your word count. Ensure that your word count adheres to the limits defined for this essay prompt.

Please work on the areas outlined above and submit another draft for review when you're ready!

Cheers,
BeMo

The following document is a final draft that was the result of multiple revisions with our admissions expert. Typically, there are two to three revisions.

2e. Final draft

How do you make a choice between the value of honesty and a risk to your fledgling career? I had to make this choice when I discovered that a senior colleague infringed copyright in external training documents, putting our company at legal risk, as well as reputational risk. Revealing this copyright infringement could have academic, professional, and personal consequences for me.

As an intern, one of my tasks was to perform a final review of training documents before sending them for printing. While reviewing the chapters prepared by my colleague, I noticed that the writing style and tone was very different from earlier chapters this colleague submitted. The discovery concerned me, and I decided to upload the new chapters to our copyright assessment tool. The report generated by the tool identified that much of the content was copied from external sources.

Copyright infringement could have extensive legal and ethical ramifications for our company. Besides the possibility of legal action by the copyright owner, there was a risk to the reputation of our company. Further, beyond legal and reputational concerns, no individual or organization has the right to use original content created by someone else and present it as their own. Copyrighted content needs to be shared responsibly, with credit to the original author, and within the requirements defined by copyright law. Adhering to copyright law ensures that copyright owners are acknowledged for their creative endeavors. Recognizing copyright owners' work is also a way to give back to the community of creators, as it introduces readers to authors, artists, and thought leaders whom they might otherwise have not encountered. Supporting the original work of these creators gives them the financial means and the audience to continue making new and innovative content that enriches our society and encourages progress.

I sincerely respect the work of content creators and the laws that protect them. As someone who discovered copyright infringement at my company, I knew it was my responsibility to inform my manager, who then directed my colleague to re-do the work.

Speaking out against one of my colleagues was one of the most difficult decisions I've ever made. It eroded my manager's trust and opinion of my colleague, which then damaged my working relationship with that colleague. Also, because I was an intern student, revealing the lapse of judgment of a senior colleague risked my internship, as well as my professional reputation. My senior colleague had an extensive network of relationships at the company, and there could be repercussions to my positive relationships with other colleagues who were close to this person. I could potentially damage my career before it even started.

When I shared damaging information about my colleague with my manager, I knew that it could have academic, professional, and personal consequences for me, but my manager assured me that I took the correct action. As expected, some of my work relationships were impacted by my decision, but I was determined to remain professional, approachable, and ethical. I hold honesty in the highest regard and felt a responsibility to adhere to my values. Being honest, regardless of the personal expense to me, was a small sacrifice to make to uphold the integrity of someone else's creative work and efforts.

2f. Discussion

This applicant shared a difficult story about choosing honesty when there was a risk of impacting their relationship with a colleague. The situation was further complicated because the applicant was a student intern at the company and the colleague was in a senior role. However, the applicant valued honesty and felt responsible for speaking up at their own personal expense about information that could potentially damage the company's reputation.

In the final draft, the applicant improved the introduction of the essay by capturing the attention of the reader with a question. Whereas the first draft simply described the applicant's internal conflict, this new approach inspires the reader's interest.

The applicant modified the essay to follow a chronological order and organized the essay into distinct paragraphs. They also improved the essay's language by making it more concise and professional, which gave the applicant room to expand on their main theme.

The final draft's revised conclusion summarizes the key points and revisits the internal conflict experienced by the applicant. The applicant takes time to consider what honesty means to them with respect to the situation described in the essay and their own internal value system.

The personal statement prompt: Describe a topic that captivates you, and why. How have you expanded your knowledge of this topic?

3a. First draft

I have always been fascinated by space. I had dreams of being an astronaut and floating high above Earth. I imagined multitudes of worlds across the galaxy and into the far reaches of the universe. I wanted to know if there was life beyond this tiny speck of dust we call planet Earth. Surely, our planet could not contain the only life in a universe of 200 billion galaxies and innumerable planets.

My love for space never left me. I love reading science fiction classics, from John Wyndham's The Day of the Triffids, to H. G. Wells' The War of the Worlds. One of science fiction's greatest writers, Octavia Butler, envisioned humans co-existing with alien species in her Xenogenesis trilogy. A contemporary author, Becky Chambers, writes optimistically about diverse groups of space travelers comprised of humans and their companions from other planets. Regardless of the author's perspective on human-alien interaction, humanity's entry into space demands deep reflection on how we will respond if we do encounter species from outside our planet.

As human technology advances, so too does the possibility that our species will move off-world or encounter other life. As a space enthusiast, I receive news notifications regularly about space technology and discoveries, and I regularly visit the NASA website. Even if these discoveries do not provide us with evidence of life elsewhere, they will give us insight into the history and life cycle of planets, as well as the formation of the universe itself.

As an armchair astronomer and an aspiring pre-med student, I do not expect to ever leave the confines of Earth, but I do plan to contribute to life here on Earth. Medical practices and technology need to address the unique considerations of humans traveling and living outside our planet.

3b. Exercise: Can you spot the errors?

Use the space below to write down the errors you have spotted. Make sure you do this before moving on to the next section. Besides identifying grammatical errors, also make note of red flags, issues with structure and flow, and so forth. Take your time and refer to *Chapter III: 7 Common Essay Errors* if necessary.

3c. List of errors

Now let's examine the errors our admissions expert identified. To help you better understand our approach, these errors will be bolded and underlined in the revised draft in the following section.

- *Weak introduction:* The introduction is not creative or engaging. The applicant can improve it by sharing a significant experience, question, or relevant quote.

- *Informal language:* Although it is not prevalent, there is one instance where the applicant uses colloquial language, which is not appropriate for a formal essay.

- *Examples need expansion:* There should be a purpose to everything included in the essay. Occasionally, the applicant mentions things that are not discussed further.

- *Weak transitions:* The transitions from one paragraph to the next are sometimes abrupt. The essay would benefit from stronger transitions between paragraphs. The topic of each paragraph should easily lead the reader to the next paragraph.

- *Too short:* This essay does not make good use of the available word count. Common App allows essays of up to 650 words long. The first draft is less than half that amount.

Note: The passages in which the expert left comments or suggestions for the student to review are underlined and marked using superscript numerals. Use these numerals to reference our expert's comments/suggestions listed below the revised draft.

3d. First revision by a BeMo admissions expert

I have always been fascinated by space.[1] I had dreams of being an astronaut and floating high above Earth. I imagined multitudes of worlds across the galaxy and into the far reaches of the universe. I wanted to know if there was life beyond this **tiny speck of dust we call planet Earth**.[2] Surely, our planet could not contain the only life in a universe of 200 billion galaxies and innumerable planets.

    My love for space never left me.[3] **I love reading science fiction classics, from John Wyndham's The Day of the Triffids, to H. G. Wells' The War of the Worlds**.[4] One of science fiction's greatest writers, Octavia Butler, envisioned humans co-existing with alien species in her Xenogenesis trilogy. A contemporary author, Becky Chambers, writes optimistically about diverse groups of space travelers comprised of humans and their companions from other planets. Regardless of the author's perspective on human-alien interaction, humanity's entry into space demands deep reflection on how we will respond if we do encounter species from outside our planet.

    As human technology advances, so too does the possibility that our species will move off-world or encounter other life. As a space enthusiast, I **receive news notifications regularly**[5] about space technology and discoveries, and **I regularly visit the NASA website**.[6] Even if these discoveries do not provide us with evidence of life elsewhere, they will give us insight into the history and life cycle of planets, as well as the formation of the universe itself.

    As an armchair astronomer and an aspiring pre-med student, I do not expect to ever leave the confines of Earth, but I do plan to contribute to life here on Earth. Medical practices and technology need to address the unique considerations of humans traveling and living outside our planet.[7]

Word count prior to revision: 295

Word count after revision: 295

Word count limit: 650

Expert's comments/suggestions:

1. Your introductory sentence needs to engage the reader, as it will be their first impression of you. Make it interesting by sharing a significant experience, question, or relevant quote.

2. Avoid wordiness, as well as cliché or colloquial language. You are writing a formal essay. Your goal is to present a polished and professional final product.

3. As a lifelong interest, it would be worthwhile to outline what captivated you about this topic as a child. This information will personalize your essay and build context for the rest of your story.

4. Rather than simply listing books you enjoy, connect the content of the books to your interest in space.

5. This wording is awkward. Use simple language.

6. Expand on specific NASA technology or projects that you follow. These types of details will demonstrate your continued interest in space as an adult.

7. Your conclusion is interesting and leaves the reader with something to ponder. However, I suggest changing the order of these sentences to end on a more powerful note that is specifically about you.

Our expert's overall feedback in the end:

Great job on your first draft! It was nice to read an essay from a fellow space enthusiast.

Your essay follows a chronological structure, which makes it easy for the reader to follow. You begin by describing your childhood love of space, but your introductory sentence is not unique or creative. I recommend starting with a specific childhood incident that truly encapsulates how this interest began for you. This will engage the reader and encourage their interest in the rest of your essay.

You spend some time in the body of your essay discussing how your childhood fascination with space translated to a love of science fiction books in adulthood. While you did a good job of expanding on these examples for contemporary authors, you didn't describe the themes that attracted you in classic science fiction novels. Including a fuller description will provide better context for the final sentence of this paragraph.

The body of your essay also alludes to NASA, but the reader would appreciate knowing more details about specific technology or processes that you follow. Remember that part of your essay prompt is about how you are expanding your knowledge of the topic.

Your conclusion is unique and memorable, aligning the values that encouraged your interest in space to the medical profession you are pursuing. However, the order of the sentences in the last paragraph should be reversed to place the final focus on you.

Your essay revisions may change your word count. Ensure that your word count adheres to the limits defined for this essay prompt.

Please work on the areas outlined above and submit another draft for review when you're ready!

Cheers,
BeMo

The following document is a final draft that was the result of multiple revisions with our admissions expert. Typically, there are two to three revisions.

3e. Final draft

One of my earliest memories is laying down in the backseat of my parent's car and staring up at the night sky through the car's rear window. I watched in awe as the stars glided by above my head, and I would pretend I was flying in a spaceship. I had dreams of being an astronaut and floating high above Earth. Space was fascinating to me. I imagined multitudes of worlds across the galaxy and into the far reaches of the universe. I wanted to know if there was life beyond the tiny speck of planet Earth. Surely, our planet could not contain the only life in a universe of 200 billion galaxies and innumerable planets.

A knowledge-hungry child, I spent countless hours watching movies about enterprising young people building spaceships in their backyards and documentaries about actual space flights. These were stories of triumphs and tragedies — from Neil Armstrong's first steps on the moon to the Challenger disaster. These intrepid explorers took incredible risks and made huge sacrifices, in some cases their lives, to launch humankind beyond the confines of our world.

My love for space and my admiration for astronauts never left me. However, as an adult, it manifested differently. While I continue to watch movies and documentaries about space, my preference now is to devour science fiction novels. I love the classics, from John Wyndham's The Day of the Triffids about otherworldly sentient plants destroying human civilization, to alien invasion in H. G. Wells' The War of the Worlds. One of science fiction's greatest writers, Octavia Butler, envisioned humans co-existing with alien species in her Xenogenesis trilogy. A contemporary author, Becky Chambers, writes optimistically about diverse groups of space travelers comprised of humans and their companions from other planets. Regardless of the author's perspective on human-alien interaction, either positive or negative, humanity's entry into space demands deep reflection on how we will respond if we do encounter species from outside our planet.

As human technology advances, so too does the possibility that our species will move off-world or encounter other life. As a space enthusiast, I regularly read news about space technology and discoveries, and I enjoy exploring the NASA website. The Mars Exploration Rover mission offers the promise of a human colony for future generations, and the James Webb telescope provides a view of galaxies that would otherwise be beyond our reach. Even if these projects do not provide us with evidence of life elsewhere, they will give us insight into the history and life cycle of planets, as well as the formation of the universe itself.

Medical practices and technology need to address the unique considerations of humans traveling and living outside our planet as companies like SpaceX work toward establishing colonies on Mars. Physicians will certainly have a part in these ventures as they look for ways to sustain life in harsh environments. As an armchair astronomer and an aspiring pre-med student, I don't expect to ever leave the confines of Earth or be part of the innovations that will propel our species off-world to the next stage of our evolution, but I do plan to contribute to the flourishing of humankind here on Earth.

3f. Discussion

The final draft of this personal statement illustrates two key improvements by the applicant: a captivating introduction and expanded descriptions of information included in the body of the essay.

The original introductory sentence lacked interest and was not designed to gain the attention of the reader. The updated introduction is longer and recalls a vivid memory from the applicant's childhood, immediately engaging the reader. This change will benefit the applicant because of the primacy effect, whereby readers tend to recall items that are presented to them first. A unique introduction will make the applicant memorable to the admissions committee.

The body of the essay has been modified to create better transitions between paragraphs, as well as expand on the details provided. The additional information develops a stronger profile of the applicant and better responds to the essay prompt.

The personal statement prompt: What interests have defined you as a person?

4a. First draft

Some say that you know when you get that warm, tingly feeling at the bottom of your stomach. Or when you think about it, you are so giddy you feel anxious. Maybe when you finally tell your friends, you have no idea where to start talking.

Growing up, I was amongst countless starry eyed girls who were in love with dance. It did not matter where I was; I loved to dance, and I was a starry-eyed dancer of two forms. One moment I was a ballet pointe performer, tiptoeing across the stage with my pink tutu swooshing around me. In another, I was a figure skater, gliding across the ice as my legs intertwined into a tight spiral spin.

I thought that I had found my perfect match. At the peak of our relationship, I won the bronze medal for figure skating in the junior division at the Wollman Open in New York. It all came to a sudden halt when one day, my parents broke the news that they could not afford any more lessons.

The next step in my journey took place sophomore year of high school; I made the varsity gymnastics team at Bronx Science, where attendance did not cost money. My dance background allowed me to adapt swiftly and soon enough, I was tumbling, twisting, and leaping alongside my teammates. After a couple weeks of grueling work, I was already competing in two events: vault and beam.

But something was not right. I dreaded every practice as the four-foot-something beam became my bitter enemy. It did not take me long to realize I was no longer competing against other athletes; I was competing against the sport.

I began to acknowledge that although our time together was short-lived, dance was the only thing that could ever give me that inexplicable feeling of warmth. Ballet and figure skating had pushed me to be a more expressive person through beautiful art forms. I was better for having them, but ready to move on.

Having lost a crucial part of my identity, I vowed to venture outside of my comfort zone to discover new passions. One such opportunity led me to apply for an internship to shadow an ophthalmologist at [removed identifier] in [removed identifier]. Instead of being expressive physically, I began training to express myself through communication; from patient care to working with other doctors, I found myself very much enjoying the ambiance of a physician's work setting.

From shadowing various ophthalmologists to assisting in administrative work at the office, I felt a new kind of excitement. I loved the experience of patient interaction and watching physicians deliver care that was tailored to each patient's unique needs. Following my three month shadowing period, I found myself using the same positive adjectives to describe my internship as I did dance. In school, my growing fondness for challenging science courses reaffirms my desire to pursue a career in the health professions.

I believe that my journey to find experiences that excite me has both physically and mentally challenged me. I am incredibly grateful for the dreams that have come my way and now, I am ready to take on this one.

4b. Exercise: Can you spot the errors?

Use the space below to write down the errors you have spotted. Make sure you do this before moving on to the next section. Besides identifying grammatical errors, also make note of red flags, issues with structure and flow, and so forth. Take your time and refer to *Chapter III: 7 Common Essay Errors* if necessary.

4c. List of errors

Now let's examine the errors our admissions expert identified. To help you better understand our approach, these errors will be bolded and underlined in the revised draft in the following section.

- *Not concise:* The applicant's wording is not always concise. Certain phrases can be reduced to fewer words while still retaining the original meaning. Concise writing is more clear and easier to read.

- *Grammar and punctuation errors:* The first paragraph consists mostly of phrases that are awkward to read. By combining phrases or rewording the text, these can be presented as full sentences. Further, some punctuation is misused, missing, or placed in the wrong location.

- *Lack of clarity:* Some sentences are missing words that can cause distraction or confusion for the reader.

- *Poor flow:* Although the overall flow and structure of the essay is logical, the flow between and within sentences is lacking. This issue can be overcome through better word choices and correcting problems with sentence structure. Additionally, the organization of the essay can be improved to support flow, such as by combining paragraphs of the same topic.

Note: **The passages in which the expert left comments or suggestions for the student to review are underlined and marked using superscript numerals. Use these numerals to reference our expert's comments/suggestions listed below the revised draft.**

4d. First revision by a BeMo admissions expert

Some say that you **know**[1] when you get that warm, tingly feeling at the bottom of your stomach**, or**[2] when you think about it, **you become** ~~you are~~[3] so giddy you feel anxious. ~~Maybe when you finally tell your friends, you have no idea where to start talking~~.[4] **Growing up, I was amongst countless starry-eyed**[5] **girls who were in love with dance**.[6] It did not matter where I was; I loved to dance, and I was a ~~starry-eyed~~[7] dancer of two forms. **One moment I was a ballet pointe performer, tiptoeing across the stage with my pink tutu swooshing around me. In another, I was a figure skater, gliding across the ice as my legs intertwined into a tight spiral spin**.[8]

I thought that I had found my perfect match **in dance**.[9] At the peak of our relationship, I won the bronze medal for figure skating in the junior division at the [removed identifier] in [removed identifier]. It all came to a sudden halt when one day, my parents broke the news that they could not afford any more lessons.

The next step in my journey took place **in my**[10] sophomore year of high school**.**[11] **I joined** ~~made~~[12] the varsity gymnastics team at [removed identifier], where attendance did not cost money. My dance background allowed me to adapt swiftly and soon enough, I was tumbling, twisting, and leaping alongside my teammates. After a couple weeks of grueling work, I was already competing in two events: vault and beam. **However, ~~But~~**[13] **something was not right. I dreaded every practice as the four-foot-something beam became my bitter enemy**.[14] It did not take me long to realize I was no longer competing against other athletes; I was competing against the sport.

I began to acknowledge that although our time together was short-lived, dance was the only thing that could ~~ever~~[15] give me that inexplicable feeling of warmth. **Ballet, figure skating, and gymnastics**[16] had pushed me to be a more expressive person through beautiful art forms. I was better for having them, but ready to move on.

Having lost a crucial part of my identity, I vowed to venture outside of my comfort zone to discover new passions. One such opportunity led me to apply for an internship to shadow an ophthalmologist at [removed identifier] in [removed identifier]. Instead of being expressive physically, I began training to express myself through communication**. From**[17] patient care to working with other doctors, I found myself very much enjoying the ambiance of a physician's work setting.

From shadowing various ophthalmologists to assisting in administrative work at the office, I felt a new kind of excitement. I loved the experience of patient interaction and watching physicians deliver care that was tailored to each patient's unique needs. Following my **three-month**[18] shadowing period, **I found myself using the same positive adjectives to describe my internship as I did dance**.[19] In school, my growing fondness for challenging science courses reaffirms my desire to pursue a career in the health professions.

~~I believe that my journey to~~ **Finding**[20] experiences that excite me has both physically and mentally challenged me. I am incredibly grateful for the dreams that have come my way**, and now**[21] I am ready to take on this one.

Word count prior to revision: 531

Word count after revision: 512

Word count limit: 650

Expert's comments/suggestions:

1. Can you clarify what you mean? What is it that you know?

2. This paragraph is comprised mostly of phrases rather than full sentences, which could be difficult for the reader to process. To help correct this error, this phrase can be combined with the first sentence, as shown.

3. After combining the first two sentences, the original wording needs to be adjusted to flow better.

4. Remove this sentence. It doesn't add any value to your essay and your meaning is not clear.

5. "Starry eyed" is a compound word describing "girls," so it should be hyphenated. Without the hyphen, your meaning may be misinterpreted by the reader.

6. This sentence and the rest of the paragraph should be combined with the initial paragraph for better flow, as shown.

7. To give your writing variety, avoid using repetitive descriptions. "Starry-eyed" was already used in the previous sentence.

8. Fantastic! These extra details add interest to your essay and engage the reader.

9. The subject of this sentence wasn't clear. Indicate that you are discussing the sport of dance, as shown.

10. This sentence was missing words, which can be distracting to the reader.

11. Change the semi-colon to a period. Semi-colons should only be used in limited circumstances to join two strongly connected sentences.

12. Use "joined" rather than "made." It's more precise.

13. Using the word "But" to start a sentence is too casual. As this is a formal essay, start your sentence with "However."

14. This paragraph continues the topic of the previous paragraph. To support flow, combine the two paragraphs into one, as shown.

15. Remove this word to improve conciseness without altering the meaning of the sentence.

16. You also described gymnastics, which should be acknowledged here, as shown, for consistency.

17. The semi-colon is unnecessary here and should be replaced with a period.

18. "Three month" is a compound word describing "shadowing period," so it should be hyphenated.

19. Great work connecting the ideas in your essay!

20. By removing some phrasing in this sentence, you make it more concise. Your reader will find the sentence easier to read, and you will gain extra space in your available word count to elaborate elsewhere.

21. Moving the comma within this sentence improves the readability.

Our expert's overall feedback in the end:

You've written a wonderful first draft! Thank you for sharing it with us for review.

I found your essay interesting and engaging. Your wording is creative and draws in the reader. However, there are places where you could be more concise. Also, ensure your sentences are grammatically correct and that you've used the proper punctuation. Minor errors in grammar and punctuation are distracting to the reader, especially when there are many of them. Be sure to review your essay in detail. Use your word processing tool's built-in editor to identify and fix any remaining errors.

One major change I recommend is to combine your first and second paragraphs. This change will improve the overall flow of your essay. These paragraphs describe the same topic, so separating them is jarring for the reader.

Your essay revisions may change your word count. Ensure that your word count adheres to the limits defined for this essay prompt.

Please work on the areas outlined above and submit another draft for review when you're ready!

Cheers,
BeMo

The following document is a final draft that was the result of multiple revisions with our admissions expert. Typically, there are two to three revisions.

4e. Final draft

Some say that you know you have found your passion when you get that warm, tingly feeling in your stomach, or when you think about it, you become so giddy you feel anxious. Growing up, I was amongst countless starry-eyed girls who were in love with dance. It did not matter where I was; I loved to dance, and I was a dancer of two forms. One moment I was a ballet pointe performer, tiptoeing across the stage with my pink tutu swooshing around me. In another, I was a figure skater, gliding across the ice as my legs intertwined into a tight spiral spin.

I thought that I had found my perfect match in dance. At my peak, I won the bronze medal for figure skating in the junior division at the [removed identifier] in [removed identifier]. It all came to a sudden halt when one day, my parents broke the news that they could not afford any more lessons.

The next step in my journey took place in my sophomore year of high school. I joined the varsity gymnastics team at [removed identifier], where attendance did not cost money. My dance background allowed me to adapt swiftly. Soon enough, I was tumbling, twisting, and leaping alongside my teammates. After a couple weeks of grueling work, I was already competing in two events: vault and beam. However, something was not right. I dreaded every practice as the four-foot-something beam became my bitter enemy. It did not take me long to realize I was no longer competing against other athletes; I was competing against the sport.

I began to acknowledge that although our time together was short-lived, dance was the only thing that could give me that inexplicable feeling of warmth. Ballet, figure skating, and gymnastics encouraged me to be a more expressive person through beautiful art forms. I was better for having them, but ready to move on.

Having lost a crucial part of my identity, I vowed to venture outside of my comfort zone to discover new passions. One such opportunity led me to apply for an internship to shadow an ophthalmologist. Instead of being expressive physically, I began training to express myself through communication. From patient care to working with other doctors, I found myself very much enjoying the ambiance of a physician's work setting.

From shadowing various ophthalmologists to assisting in administrative work at the office, I felt a new kind of excitement. I loved the experience of patient interaction and watching physicians deliver care that was tailored to each patient's unique needs. Following my three-month shadowing period, I found myself using the same positive adjectives to describe my internship as I did dance. In school, my growing fondness for challenging science courses reaffirms my desire to pursue a career in the health professions.

Finding experiences that excite me has both physically and mentally challenged me. I am incredibly grateful for the dreams that have come my way, and now I am ready to take on this one.

4f. Discussion

While this applicant's initial draft was creative and engaging, several grammatical and punctuation errors detracted from its effectiveness. Further, areas lacking concise wording reduced the ease of reading and clarity of the essay. In the final draft, the applicant reorganized the flow of the initial paragraphs, adjusted the wording for conciseness and clarity, and removed grammatical and punctuation errors. In their final draft, the applicant accomplished an engaging and polished essay.

The personal statement prompt: Think about a significant educational experience. How did it encourage your enthusiasm for learning?

5a. First draft

Over the past two years, I have had the opportunity to participate in a large scale research project on heat acclimation, as well as a review on treatment of exercise-induced hyperthermia. These projects have allowed me to gain valuable experience recruiting participants, working with novel laboratory equipment, extensive data analysis, and manuscripts.

I am examining how the body's physiological capacity to dissipate heat changes during and following short-term heat acclimation. Following a series of pilot trials, my supervisor and I adapted a novel experimental paradigm that was first used to assess differences in sudomotor capacity between males and females to examine how maximal sudomotor capacity changes as a function of heat acclimation. Subsequently, I have taken the lead role in the data collection and data analysis of the project. Since my data collection is still underway, I have not had the chance to publish any of my findings in peer reviewed journals. Nonetheless, I have submitted abstracts to the [removed identifier] Conference held by the [removed identifier], as well as the [removed identifier] Conference hosted by the [removed identifier] Society in order to present my findings to a large number of health professionals and contribute significantly to the scientific community.

Apart from this project, I have been very involved in the research community. I have helped with various other studies aimed at evaluating the mechanisms of post-exercise hypotension in trained and untrained males; the effects of aging and type 2 diabetes on the ability to dissipate heat to the environment; as well as biophysical considerations of whole-body cooling following exercise-induced hyperthermia. These opportunities have given me the chance to explore and work with some of the innovative and unique research tools available in [removed identifier]'s laboratory. Such equipment includes the use of the whole-body modified Snellen direct calorimeter, which allows for direct measurement of whole-body heat loss. In addition to the training I have received, I have been fortunate to have worked alongside great people that have been instrumental in increasing my knowledge and comprehension of human thermoregulation. Their demonstrated hard work and passion for advancing knowledge have been important in my decision to further develop my research skills in this field of research.

My research experience has helped me develop a better understanding of the limitations to working in hot environments. Considering that many occupations require employees to work long hours under thermally challenging conditions, it is essential to further our knowledge of how the human body adapts to these environments and how this may change as a function of age and/or health status. My proposed research will focus on advancing our knowledge of the mechanisms that govern our body's capacity to adapt to the heat, which will contribute to the safety of vulnerable populations.

5b. Exercise: Can you spot the errors?

Use the space below to write down the errors you have spotted. Make sure you do this before moving on to the next section. Besides identifying grammatical errors, also make note of red flags, issues with structure and flow, and so forth. Take your time and refer to *Chapter III: 7 Common Essay Errors* if necessary.

5c. List of errors

Now let's examine the errors our admissions expert identified. To help you better understand our approach, these errors will be bolded and underlined in the revised draft in the following section.

- *Weak introduction:* The introduction is not unique and will not stand apart from the essays of other applicants. Describing a transformative interaction, asking a question, or sharing a quote are different strategies the applicant could use to improve their introductory sentence.

- *Examples need expansion:* Although the applicant describes many details about their research project, they have not revealed why the project makes them excited about learning. Taking time to reflect on the prompt will also personalize the essay and engage the reader.

- *Need for condensing:* This essay contains very technical information that the reader may not comprehend. By simplifying and summarizing the wording, the applicant can reflect more fully on the essay prompt.

- *Grammatical errors:* There are words missing in a few places. It is important to review the essay in entirety to catch these errors before submitting.

- *Weak conclusion:* The conclusion lacks creativity and is not memorable. The essay would benefit from a strong concluding sentence to leave the reader with a positive and memorable impression.

- *Too short:* The Common App system allows a word count range of 250 to 650 words. The initial draft of this essay is 455 words long. The essay would benefit from the expansion of some ideas.

<u>Note</u>: **The passages in which the expert left comments or suggestions for the student to review are underlined and marked using superscript numerals. Use these numerals to reference our expert's comments/suggestions listed below the revised draft.**

5d. First revision by a BeMo admissions expert

Over the past two years, I have had the opportunity to participate in a **large-scale**[1] research project on heat acclimation, as well as **conduct**[2] a review on **the**[3] treatment of exercise-induced hyperthermia. These projects have allowed me to gain valuable experience recruiting participants, working with novel laboratory equipment, **analyzing extensive data sets** ~~analysis~~,[4] and **developing manuscripts** ~~development~~.[5]

I am examining how the body's physiological capacity to dissipate heat changes during and following short-term heat acclimation. Following a series of pilot trials, my supervisor and I adapted a novel experimental paradigm that was first used to **assess differences in sudomotor capacity between males and females to examine how maximal sudomotor capacity changes as a function of heat acclimation**.[6] Subsequently, I have taken the lead role in the data collection and data analysis of the project. Since my data collection is still underway, I have not had the chance to publish any of my findings in **peer-reviewed**[7] journals. **Nonetheless, I have submitted abstracts to the [removed identifier] Conference held by the [removed identifier],[8] as well as the [removed identifier] Conference hosted by the [removed identifier] Society in order to present my findings to a large number of health professionals and contribute significantly to the scientific community.**[9]

Apart from this project, I have been very involved in the research community. **I have helped with various other studies aimed at evaluating the mechanisms of post-exercise hypotension in trained and untrained males; the effects of aging and type 2 diabetes on the ability to dissipate heat to the environment; as well as biophysical considerations of whole-body cooling following exercise-induced hyperthermia. These opportunities have given me the chance to explore and work with some of the innovative and unique research tools available in [removed identifier]'s laboratory. Such equipment includes the use of the whole-body modified Snellen direct**

calorimeter, which allows for direct measurement of whole-body heat loss.[10] In addition to the training I have received, I have been fortunate to have worked alongside great people that have been instrumental in increasing my knowledge and comprehension of human thermoregulation. Their demonstrated hard work and passion for advancing knowledge have been important in my decision to further develop my research skills in this field ~~of research~~.[11]

My research experience has helped me develop a better understanding of the limitations **of** ~~to~~[12] working in hot environments. Considering that many occupations require employees to work long hours under thermally challenging conditions, it is essential to further our knowledge of how the human body adapts to these environments and how this may change as a function of **age, ~~and/or~~ health status, or both**.[13] My proposed research will focus on advancing our knowledge of the mechanisms that govern our body's capacity to adapt to the heat, which will contribute to the safety of vulnerable populations.

Word count prior to revision: 456

Word count after revision: 457

Word count limit: 650

Expert's comments/suggestions:

1. This compound word needs to be hyphenated. Be sure to review your essay in detail, as well as using your word processor's built-in editor, to locate these types of errors before finalizing your essay.

2. This sentence was missing a word ("conduct") that impacts clarity. As a best practice, always read through your document completely before submitting it.

3. A word is also missing here ("the"), which impacts the readability of the sentence.

4. When you list items separated by commas, use parallel structure so that each item in the list follows a consistent structure.

5. This list item also does not follow parallel structure. Update this phrase to match the other items in the list.

6. This sentence is quite wordy. Look for opportunities to simplify your language, sharing the main ideas but not details that aren't critical to answering the essay prompt.

7. This compound word needs to be hyphenated.

8. A comma is required here. Using the correct punctuation gives your essay a polished and professional presentation.

9. This information can be reduced. Look for opportunities to make your essay concise while still sharing the key points.

10. While it's important to provide some details to give the reader the appropriate context, too much complexity will make your essay inaccessible to the reader. Maintain your focus on the learning you have achieved as opposed to the specific technical details of the research project.

11. The wording here is repetitive. Watch for this type of issue when you complete your final review as repetition can be distracting to the reader.

12. The correct word to use is "of" rather than "to."

13. Avoid using "and/or" as it's not precise and can cause confusion for the reader.

Our expert's overall feedback in the end:

Your research project sounds like an amazing learning experience. Thank you for sharing it with us!

Your introduction is the most important part of the essay. The reader will develop their first impression of you at the start, so the introduction must be compelling. Try describing a transformative interaction, asking a question, or sharing a quote to make your introduction stand out.

The body of your essay is ripe with details about your research project. While this information is important to provide context, be sure to focus your time on responding to the essay prompt. The admissions committee wants to know how this experience made you enthusiastic about learning, not as much the specific details of that learning.

Like the introduction, your concluding statement also needs to make an impression. Ensure it is memorable.

Finally, ensure you always review your essay and use your word processor's built-in editor to catch any mistakes in grammar, punctuation, or spelling.

Although these errors are typically minor, they can be distracting and indicate to the reader that you didn't take time or care with your essay before submitting it.

Your essay revisions may change your word count. Ensure that your word count adheres to the limits defined for this essay prompt.

Please work on the areas outlined above and submit another draft for review when you're ready!

Cheers,
BeMo

The following document is a final draft that was the result of multiple revisions with our admissions expert. Typically, there are two to three revisions.

5e. Final draft

Have you ever wondered how the human body reacts to heat? The ability of the human body to conform or not conform to its environment has long been an interest of mine, especially as a person who has grown up in the era of climate change. Over the past two years, I have had the opportunity to participate in a research project on heat acclimation, as well as conduct a review on the treatment of exercise-induced hyperthermia. I am examining how the body's physiological capacity to dissipate heat changes during and following short-term heat acclimation. My profound learnings related to this project have been immense and varied. Besides taking a lead role in data collection and analysis, I have also submitted abstracts to various conferences to present my findings, thereby contributing significantly to the scientific community.

This project has inspired an increased enthusiasm for learning and enticed me to become involved in the research community. I have helped with other studies related to post-exercise hypotension in trained and untrained males, the effects of aging and type 2 diabetes on the ability to dissipate heat to the environment, and biophysical considerations of whole-body cooling following exercise-induced hyperthermia. These studies have given me the chance to explore and work with innovative research tools, such as the Snellen direct calorimeter, which allows for direct measurement of whole-body heat loss.

I have been fortunate to have worked alongside great people that have been instrumental in increasing my knowledge and comprehension of human thermoregulation. Their hard work and passion for advancing knowledge have been important in my desire to further develop my skills in this field. In particular, Dr. [removed identifier], has always taken the time to guide me through my research project. His constant dedication to his students offers an incredible learning environment that I feel is also reflected in the culture and values at [removed identifier], where I would like to continue my studies.

This research experience has given me a better understanding of the limitations of working in hot environments, especially in a time of rapid climate change and significant overall increases in the earth's temperatures. Considering that many occupations require employees to work long hours under thermally challenging conditions, it is essential for humanity to further our knowledge of how the body adapts to these environments and how the body's regulation may change as a function of age, health status, or both. With aspirations to eventually work in developing countries to contribute to innovations in this area, my next focus is advancing my knowledge of the body's capacity to adapt to heat, which will contribute to the safety of our world's most vulnerable populations.

Through this project and its associated educational experience, I reconfirmed that research is my passion and will give me a means to pursue a goal of lifelong learning. The study of heat acclimation is essential for guiding human adaptation to climate change and has the potential for major impacts to populations globally. Learning more about the human body's acclimation to heat, as well as contributing to solutions that minimize the negative effects of climate change on the human body, will give me the rare privilege of making a lasting improvement in the lives of current and future generations.

5f. Discussion

The applicant's revisions to their essay made it a more powerful, compelling personal statement. In particular, the applicant used a question to entice the reader's interest at the beginning of the essay. This approach will help make the applicant stand out to the admissions committee.

Another key change made by the applicant was to remove the focus from project details to how the project inspired the applicant's enthusiasm for learning. This change was critical for the final draft as the essay needs to answer the essay prompt. The original draft did not adequately provide this information.

In the final draft, the applicant took care to review their essay in detail, which allowed them to address minor punctuation and grammatical errors.

Finally, the concluding statement is memorable and leaves the reader with a positive impression of the applicant.

The personal statement prompt: Describe an obstacle you faced. What did you learn from overcoming this obstacle, and how will you apply this learning to future challenges?

6a. First draft

At 8 years old, my parents took me to an educational psychologist as they had concerns about my capacity to learn. Prior to this assessment, I presented with speech delays and motor skills impairment. I had trouble with pronunciation, and I could not grasp a pencil correctly when first learning to print. I received support in my early school years for these difficulties and made significant improvements, but other learning delays cropped up.

In particular, I could not focus in class and it was nearly impossible for me to retain information. My teacher moved me to the front of the classroom, but it did not make much difference. I found myself constantly distracted by other students or activities occurring outside the classroom, in the hallway, or outside the window. Despite the fact that I was not learning anything, my teachers continued to pass me into the next grade every year, which put me further behind as the content was becoming increasingly more difficult.

Although my assessment with the educational psychologist recommended extra school support for me, school budgets only allowed for me to get extra help for about an hour a week, which was not enough time to be valuable for me. My teachers met with my parents regularly to try to find solutions, but the strategies put in place made little difference to my results. My teachers and parents were becoming frustrated, and so was I. My challenges were also affecting my interactions with my classmates.

In Grade 5, my parents took me out of the school system and started homeschooling me. This decision was illuminating for them. They discovered that my work was only at a Grade 1 level, so I had a lot of catching up to do. Despite the financial implications, my mother quit her job so that she could work with me. Certainly, we had difficult days when I was not engaged or produced sloppy work, but the one-to-one time was exactly what I needed. I improved in all areas, especially in the critical subjects of math and language arts.

Dealing with ADHD taught me so much about myself. As a person with ADHD, I need to leverage my challenges as strengths. Although I can get distracted easily, my ADHD also means that I have incredible focus and attention to detail for topics that interest me. I am an extremely high performer in these situations, even though overall I tend to perform below average. Through the experience of homeschooling, I developed important strategies for learning successfully. I know that I do better work in the morning after having had a good night's sleep, and I know that I have to complete tasks in small steps that achieve a goal. These goals could be as simple as completing one page of math, or as complex as planning and writing an essay in manageable chunks rather than attempting to write the entire draft in one sitting.

I reflected deeply on my passions when choosing a program of study. As a person with ADHD, choosing the right program is essential to whether I will excel or not. I know that I have selected the right program because I feel excited at the prospect of beginning my education, and this feeling of passion is essential for me to succeed at something.

6b. Exercise: Can you spot the errors?

Use the space below to write down the errors you have spotted. Make sure you do this before moving on to the next section. Besides identifying grammatical errors, also make note of red flags, issues with structure and flow, and so forth. Take your time and refer to *Chapter III: 7 Common Essay Errors* if necessary.

6c. List of errors

Now let's examine the errors our admissions expert identified. To help you better understand our approach, these errors will be bolded and underlined in the revised draft in the following section.

- *Weak introduction:* The introduction is not engaging and will not make the essay stand out from those of other applicants. Strategies such as opening with a question, sharing a meaningful quote, or describing a transformative experience are excellent ways of gaining the reader's interest from the start.

- *Informal language:* There are a few occasions where the applicant uses colloquial, cliché, or informal language. Removing or replacing this language will lend to a more professional overall tone.

- *Not concise:* The applicant can remove some words and phrases to make their essay more concise. This change will also provide the benefit of increasing their available word count for use elsewhere.

- *Examples need expansion:* The applicant included two statements that were not directly related to the other points in their essay. These statements need to be expanded upon to support the message of the essay. Otherwise, they should be removed.

- *Ineffective or weak transitions:* The applicant could make some improvements to their transitions between sentences and paragraphs. In particular, the start of the essay would benefit from being presented in a chronological order, and the body of the essay needs stronger transitions between one paragraph and the next.

- *Weak conclusion:* The concluding sentence does not incorporate the obstacle and learning concepts from the essay prompt. It is important to highlight these concepts in your concluding paragraph as it reaffirms to the reader that you have fully answered the questions in the prompt.

<u>Note</u>: **The passages in which the expert left comments or suggestions for the student to review are underlined and marked using superscript numerals. Use these numerals to reference our expert's comments/suggestions listed below the revised draft.**

6d. First revision by a BeMo admissions expert

<u>At 8 years old, my parents took me to an educational psychologist as they had concerns about my capacity to learn.</u>[1] **<u>Prior to this assessment,</u>**[2] I presented with speech delays and motor skills impairment. I had trouble with pronunciation, and I could not grasp a pencil correctly when first learning to print. I received support in my early school years for these difficulties and made significant improvements, but other learning delays **<u>cropped up</u>**.[3]

<u>In particular, I could not focus in class and it was nearly impossible for me to retain information.</u>[4] My teacher moved me to the front of the classroom, but it did not make much difference. I found myself constantly distracted by other students or activities occurring ~~outside the classroom,~~ **<u>in the hallway,</u>** ~~,~~ **<u>or outside the window</u>**.[5] Despite the fact that I was not learning **<u>much</u>** ~~anything~~,[6] my teachers continued to **<u>advance</u>** ~~pass~~[7] me into the next grade every year, which put me further behind as the content was becoming increasingly more difficult.

Although my assessment with the educational psychologist recommended extra school support for me, school budgets only allowed for me to get extra help for ~~about~~[8] an hour a week, which was not enough time to be valuable for me. My teachers met with my parents regularly ~~to try to~~[9] find solutions, but the strategies put in place made little difference to my results. My teachers and parents were becoming frustrated, and so was I. **<u>My challenges were also affecting my interactions with my classmates.</u>**[10]

In Grade 5, my parents took me out of the school system and started homeschooling me. This decision was illuminating for them. They discovered that my work was only at a Grade 1 level, so I had a lot of catching up to do. **<u>Despite the financial implications, my mother quit her job so that she could work with me.</u>**[11] Certainly, we had difficult days when I was not engaged or produced **<u>sloppy work</u>**,[12] but the one-to-one time was exactly what I needed. I improved in all areas, especially in the critical subjects of math and language arts.

Dealing with ADHD taught me so much about myself. As a person with ADHD, I need to leverage my challenges as strengths. Although I can get distracted easily, my ADHD also means that I have incredible focus and attention to detail for topics that interest me. I am an extremely high performer in these situations~~, even though overall I tend to perform below average~~.[13] Through the experience of homeschooling, I developed important strategies for learning successfully. I know that I do better work in the morning after having had a good night's sleep, and I know that I **must** ~~have to~~[14] complete tasks in small steps that achieve a goal. These goals could be as simple as completing one page of math, or as complex as planning and writing an essay in manageable **parts** ~~chunks~~[15] rather than attempting to write the entire draft in one sitting.

I reflected deeply on my passions when choosing a program of study. As a person with ADHD, choosing the right program is essential to whether I will excel or not. **I know that I have selected the right program because I feel excited at the prospect of beginning my education, and this feeling of passion is essential for me to succeed at something.**[16]

Word count prior to revision: 546

Word count after revision: 529

Word count limit: 650

Expert's comments/suggestions:

1. Spend some time to make your introductory sentence more unique and creative. The admissions committee will be more likely to recall your essay if your opening is memorable.

2. In the previous sentence, you discuss an experience when you were 8 years old, but this sentence discusses a time before that experience without any transition. Consider reorganizing your sentences so that they follow a chronological order. This modified structure will allow the reader to process the essay content more easily.

3. Avoid using cliché or colloquial language. Formal essays require a professional tone.

4. The wording used in this sentence refers to the final sentence of the previous paragraph, which might confuse the reader. They won't expect to see a new paragraph here. However, it is clear from the rest of the paragraph that you are beginning a new topic. Rewriting this sentence and removing "In particular" from the start of the sentence should alleviate transition issues between this paragraph and the previous paragraph.

5. Some of this wording is redundant. You don't need to refer to outside the classroom because that's suggested when you mention the hallway and outside the window. This essay has a word count limit, so look for opportunities to remove unnecessary words or phrases to give you room to expand on other key points.

6. The word "much" is more precise here as you were probably gaining some learning, even if it didn't meet grade-level expectations.

7. The word "advance" is more precise here. "Pass" has multiple meanings, so that wording might confuse readers.

8. Remove this unnecessary word to make your essay more concise.

9. This phrase can be removed for conciseness without impacting your meaning. These words aren't needed.

10. This sentence doesn't relate to the other content in your essay. Delete it so that you can divert more space to your key points.

11. Expand this statement further to explain what you learned from your mother's choice. Currently, this statement is not connected with the other ideas in your essay.

12. Avoid cliché or colloquial language to maintain a professional tone in your essay.

13. To create a positive impression for your reader, avoid negative statements. Your essay should be optimistic and focus on your strengths instead of your weaknesses.

14. Reducing your words will make your essay more concise and increase your available word count.

15. Avoid cliché or colloquial language to maintain a professional tone in your essay.

16. The essay prompt emphasizes obstacles and learning. Be sure to incorporate these concepts in your concluding sentence, while maintaining a positive and optimistic tone.

Our expert's overall feedback in the end:

Your response to the prompt is well written and shows that you took time and care in creating it.

To improve your essay, I recommend applying a creative strategy to your opening sentence to engage the reader. For example, by opening with a question, sharing a meaningful quote, or describing a transformative experience, you gain the attention of the reader immediately. It's important to make a strong impression early in your essay to differentiate you from other applicants.

The body of your essay is strong and contains many details necessary for context. However, on a few occasions you use informal language that should be removed or replaced to establish a professional tone in your essay. There are also opportunities to remove unnecessary words and phrases, which will make your essay more concise. Keep in mind that you have a word count limit of 650 words, so using concise language will ensure that you are using your space effectively.

As you are working on your final draft, carefully consider transitions between sentences and between paragraphs. Each sentence and paragraph should clearly and logically lead to the next. Although each paragraph should focus on a distinct topic, it should naturally lead from the paragraph that precedes it.

There are two statements in the body of your essay that did not directly relate to other points. I recommend expanding upon these statements in support of your overall message. Otherwise, they should be removed.

You have a good basis for your conclusion, but be sure to incorporate the obstacle and learning concepts from the essay prompt. By connecting back to the prompt, the reader is reassured that you have fully answered the question.

Your essay revisions may change your word count. Ensure that your word count adheres to the limits defined for this essay prompt.

Please work on the areas outlined above and submit another draft for review when you're ready!

Cheers,
BeMo

The following document is a final draft that was the result of multiple revisions with our admissions expert. Typically, there are two to three revisions.

6e. Final draft

Imagine sitting in the center of a classroom with people all around you. The person in front of you is tapping their pencil on their desk. The person behind you is eating a granola bar, crinkling the wrapper and chewing loudly. The person on your left is talking to a classmate, while the person on your right is coughing repeatedly. There is further chatter and noise in the room beyond them. As a person with ADHD, this environment is a cacophony of sounds.

Growing up, I could not focus during class and it was nearly impossible for me to retain information. My teacher moved me to the front of the classroom, but it did not make much difference. I was constantly distracted by other students in the classroom, the hallway, or outside the window. I was not learning much, but my teachers continued to advance me into the next grade every year.

My parents eventually took me to an educational psychologist as they had concerns about my capacity to learn. Although the assessment recommended extra school support for my ADHD, school budgets only allowed for me to get extra help for an hour a week, which was not sufficient. My teachers met with my parents regularly to discuss solutions, but the strategies made little difference to my results. My teachers and parents were becoming frustrated, and so was I.

In Grade 5, my parents took me out of the school system and started homeschooling me. My mother resigned from her job so that she could work with me. She discovered that my work was only at a Grade 1 level, so I had a lot of catching up to do. Certainly, we had difficult days when I was not engaged or produced poor work, but the one-to-one time was exactly what I needed. I improved in all areas, especially in the core subjects of math and language arts.

Managing ADHD has taught me so much about myself. As a person with ADHD, I need to leverage my strengths. Although I can get distracted easily, my ADHD also means that I have incredible focus and attention to detail for topics that interest me. I am an extremely high performer when studying these topics.

Through the experience of homeschooling, I developed important strategies for learning successfully. I know that my work is better in the morning after having had a good night's sleep, and I know that I must complete tasks in small steps that achieve a goal. These goals could be as simple as completing one page of math, or as complex as planning and writing an essay in manageable parts rather than attempting to write the entire draft in one sitting.

My biggest obstacle is identifying learning that appeals to me and captures my undivided attention. I reflected deeply on my passions when choosing a program of study. As a person with ADHD, choosing the right program is essential to whether I will excel or not. I know that I have selected the right program because I feel excited at the prospect of beginning my education, and this feeling of passion is essential for me to succeed.

6f. Discussion

The applicant successfully incorporated the feedback in the final draft of their essay. Their introduction is much stronger and inspires the reader to engage with the text. The applicant has also improved upon the body of their essay by removing unnecessary words, phrases, and sentences, as well as expanding appropriate examples to support the overall discussion. In addition, the applicant removed informal language to establish a professional tone in their essay. The concluding paragraph has been improved by referring to the obstacle and learning concepts from the essay prompt.

The improvements to this essay will help differentiate this applicant from competing candidates.

The personal statement prompt: Discuss an experience that contributed to your personal growth. How did this experience change your perception of yourself?

7a. First draft

As an aspiring engineer, I was excited to be invited to participate in my school's solar car challenge team in high school. What is the solar car challenge? This STEM program gives students the opportunity to learn new science and technology skills by designing and building a functioning solar car. I found many academic and personal benefits as a member of the solar car team.

Professionally, I have plans to become a software engineer. Designing a roadworthy solar car with the necessary software components would not only give me a practical opportunity to confirm that software engineering was the right career for me, but it would also allow me to develop engineering skills in advance of my academic pursuits. My greatest learning from this experience is that engineers do not work in isolation. It takes a team of engineers working together to build a functioning product. Our team's solar car required me to be proficient not only in my area of software engineering, but also knowledgeable about how my work on the project integrated with electrical, mechanical, material, and safety considerations. I learned skills outside of software engineering, which will help me in my academic studies.

The solar car competition has also improved my soft skills in collaboration, teamwork, problem-solving, and leadership. This in-depth project emphasized collaboration. To build a solar car requires the input, knowledge, skills, and innovation of all members of the team. If my work wasn't aligned with the work of other members of the team, then the final product would be unsuccessful. My team met regularly to discuss issues, solve problems, and design improvements. The competition was not so much about winning against other teams as it was about meeting our own goals and expectations.

Leadership was the biggest takeaway I had from participating in this experience. Because I was one of the first students to join the team, I had the opportunity to participate in interviews to select the remaining team members. Then, as the project progressed, I had more and more opportunities to contribute my knowledge and insight, as well as provide recommendations specific to the software engineering portion of the project. These leadership skills will benefit me in all aspects of my future life, whether personal or professional.

I believe that personal growth is tied not only to knowledge and skills, but also values. The solar car challenge gave me a way to contribute my ideas for environmentally friendly vehicle design to replace gas-powered transportation. The sun is an amazing source of sustainable energy that we should make better use of to power our world, not just for transportation, but for other uses such as heating our buildings and supporting food production innovations.

My participation in the solar car competition has benefited me academically and personally. I gained technical skills in software, electrical, and mechanical engineering, as well as knowledge of material and safety implications. From a soft skills perspective, I improved my collaboration, teamwork, problem-solving, and leadership skills. The solar car competition confirmed my interest in software engineering as a career, as well as giving me the foundational skills to be an innovator and leader as I continue my education and beyond.

7b. Exercise: Can you spot the errors?

Use the space below to write down the errors you have spotted. Make sure you do this before moving on to the next section. Besides identifying grammatical errors, also make note of red flags, issues with structure and flow, and so forth. Take your time and refer to *Chapter III: 7 Common Essay Errors* if necessary.

7c. List of errors

Now let's examine the errors our admissions expert identified. To help you better understand our approach, these errors will be bolded and underlined in the revised draft in the following section.

- *Poor word choice and phrasing:* Some words are not used correctly or are imprecise. The applicant needs to replace these words to ensure that the reader understands the applicant's intended meaning.

- *Lack of connection between ideas:* A few statements are isolated and do not align with the rest of the content in the essay. These statements require elaboration or removal from the essay.

- *Poor structure:* The paragraphs are not organized in a logical way. By moving sentences to other paragraphs and adding effective transition statements, the applicant will improve the overall flow of the essay.

- *Weak conclusion:* The conclusion is not memorable and will not help this applicant stand out from other candidates. The concluding statement should be rewritten with a unique or creative approach.

<u>Note</u>: **The passages in which the expert left comments or suggestions for the student to review are underlined and marked using superscript numerals. Use these numerals to reference our expert's comments/suggestions listed below the revised draft.**

7d. First revision by a BeMo admissions expert

As an aspiring engineer, I was excited to be invited to participate ~~in~~ **on**[1] my school's solar car challenge team in high school. **What is the solar car challenge?**[2] This STEM program gives students the opportunity to learn new science and technology skills by designing and building a functioning solar car. I ~~found~~ **gained**[3] many academic and personal benefits as a member of the solar car team.

Professionally, I have plans to become a software engineer. Designing a roadworthy solar car with the necessary software components would not only give me a practical opportunity to confirm that software engineering was the right career for me, but it would also allow me to develop engineering skills in advance of my **academic pursuits.**[4] **My greatest learning from this experience is that engineers do not work in isolation.**[5] It takes a team of engineers working together to build a functioning product. Our team's solar car required me to be proficient not only in my area of software engineering, but also knowledgeable about how my work on the project integrated with electrical, mechanical, material, and safety considerations. I learned skills outside of software engineering, which will help me in my academic studies.

The solar car competition has also improved my soft skills in collaboration, teamwork, problem-solving, and leadership. This in-depth project emphasized collaboration. To build a solar car requires the input, knowledge, skills, and innovation of all members of the team. If my work wasn't aligned with the work of other members of the team, then the final product would be unsuccessful. My team met regularly to discuss issues, solve problems, and design improvements. The competition was not so much about winning against other teams as it was about meeting our ~~own~~ **personal**[6] goals and expectations.

Leadership was the biggest **takeaway**[7] I had from participating in this experience. Because I was one of the first students to join the team, I had the opportunity to **participate**[8] in interviews to select the remaining team members. Then, as the project progressed, I had more ~~and more~~[9] **opportunities**[10] to contribute my knowledge and insight, as well as provide recommendations specific to the software engineering portion of the project. These leadership skills will benefit me in all aspects of my future life, whether personal or professional.

I believe that personal growth is tied not only to knowledge and skills, but also values. The solar car challenge gave me a way to contribute my ideas for environmentally friendly vehicle design to replace gas-powered transportation. **The sun is an amazing source of sustainable energy that we should make better use of to power our world, not just for transportation, but for other uses such as heating our buildings and supporting food production innovations.**[11]

My participation in the solar car competition has benefited me academically and personally. I gained technical skills in software, electrical, and mechanical engineering, as well as knowledge of material and safety implications. From a soft skills perspective, I improved my collaboration, teamwork, problem-solving, and leadership skills. **The solar car competition confirmed my interest in software engineering as a career,**[12]**as well as giving me the foundational skills to be an innovator and leader as I continue my education and beyond.**[13]

Word count prior to revision: 530

Word count after revision: 527

Word count limit: 650

Expert's comments/suggestions:

1. The correct word to use is "on" rather than "in."

2. Consider using this question to begin your essay. Asking a question is an effective way to gain your reader's attention from the start.

3. The word "gained" is more precise than "found" in this context.

4. This phrase would benefit from clarification. Are you referring to your post-secondary education?

5. This sentence discusses a new idea. A new paragraph should start here.

6. The word "own" is vague. If you mean the individual goals of each team member, then "personal goals" would be the appropriate wording.

7. Avoid cliché or colloquial language. As this is considered an academic essay, opt for formal wording.

8. A form of this word was used in the previous sentence. To avoid repetitiveness, replace this word with a different word. There are many online thesauruses available if you are having difficulty finding an alternative.

9. Aim for concise phrasing. These words do not add information or value to your essay.

10. You frequently use forms of the word "opportunity" in your essay. Use a thesaurus to find other words that represent this concept.

11. This sentence seems out of place and doesn't align with the other content in your essay. Consider removing this statement unless you can elaborate on it.

12. Consider expanding this statement to mention your interest in environmentally friendly solutions. You briefly discuss this value in the previous paragraph, but you do not trace back to it in the conclusion.

13. Your concluding statement is not creative and won't leave a lasting impression with the reader. Spend some time developing a memorable ending for your essay.

Our expert's overall feedback in the end:

Thanks for submitting your essay for review. You've made a great start!

Two important areas to prioritize in your essay are your introduction and conclusion. People tend to remember the first and last things they read, so these two parts of your essay need to be interesting and memorable. I recommend moving the question in your introduction so that it appears as the first sentence of the essay. Starting with a question is an effective way to immediately engage the reader. In your conclusion, I suggest adding another sentence to sum up your essay in a creative way.

You have wonderful details in your essay about the tasks you performed for the solar car challenge, but this information is not always clear to follow. Your essay would benefit from some paragraph reorganization, as well as an end-to-end review to ensure that you are using appropriate wording. Avoid informal or imprecise wording. Instead, aim for a professional tone. Also, be sure to fully expand on your points. Your essay should only include information that supports your response to the essay prompt. Remove any statements that don't achieve this goal.

Your essay revisions may change your word count. Ensure that your word count adheres to the limits defined for this essay prompt.

Please work on the areas outlined above and submit another draft for review when you're ready!

Cheers,
BeMo

The following document is a final draft that was the result of multiple revisions with our admissions expert. Typically, there are two to three revisions.

7e. Final draft

What is the solar car challenge? This STEM program gives students the opportunity to learn science and technology skills through designing and building a functioning solar car. As an aspiring engineer, I was excited to participate on my school's solar car team in high school, which also contributed greatly to my personal growth.

Being a member of the solar car team has provided me with many academic and personal benefits. Academically, I have plans to study engineering with a specialization in software. Designing a roadworthy solar car with the necessary software components not only gave me a practical opportunity to confirm that this was the right career for me, but it also allowed me to develop a wide range of engineering skills in advance of my post-secondary education. I learned skills outside of software engineering that I anticipate will help me in my studies. Designing our team's solar car required me to be proficient not only in software engineering, but also knowledgeable about how my work on the project integrated with electrical, mechanical, material, and safety considerations. I learned that engineers do not work in isolation. It takes a team of engineers working together to build a functioning product.

The solar car competition has also improved my soft skills in collaboration, teamwork, problem-solving, and leadership. This in-depth project emphasized collaboration. To build a solar car requires the input, knowledge, skills, and innovation of all members of the team. If my work wasn't aligned with the work of other members of the team, then the final product would be unsuccessful. My team met regularly to discuss issues, solve problems, and design improvements. The competition was not so much about winning against other teams as it was about meeting our personal goals and expectations.

The greatest benefit I obtained from the solar car challenge was leadership experience. Because I was one of the first students to join the team, I interviewed and selected the remaining team members. Then, as the project progressed, I had more opportunities to contribute my knowledge and insight, as well as share my recommendations specific to the software engineering portion of the project. These leadership skills will be an advantage in all aspects of my future life, whether personal or professional.

I believe that personal growth is tied not only to the development of knowledge and skills, but also values. The solar car challenge gave me a way to contribute my ideas for environmentally friendly vehicle design to replace gas-powered transportation. My participation on the solar car team meant that I could be part of the effort to find sustainable solutions for the future.

As a solar car team member, I gained technical skills in software, electrical, and mechanical engineering, as well as knowledge of material and safety implications. From a soft skills perspective, I improved my collaboration, teamwork, problem-solving, and leadership skills. Besides confirming my interest in software engineering as a career, the solar car competition gave me the foundational skills to be an innovator and leader in environmental sustainability, thus contributing immensely to my personal growth. The future of transportation is now: my participation in the solar car challenge made an impact to myself and the world.

7f. Discussion

The applicant's first draft included excellent information in response to the prompt, but improvements were needed to the introduction, conclusion, and organization of the essay. The introduction and conclusion were not compelling or memorable, and the body of the essay required reorganization, better transitions, attention to word choices, and reconsideration of content that did not relate directly to the essay prompt.

In the final draft, the applicant begins their essay with a question to engage the reader from the start. Similarly, the applicant includes a compelling and memorable concluding statement. These changes will set this essay apart and help differentiate it from essays submitted by other candidates.

Paragraph reorganization and better transitions support the flow of the essay in its final draft. Additionally, the applicant makes better word choices. Content in the first draft that did not fully relate to the essay prompt is absent or expanded in the final draft. The essay is now polished, professional, and concise.

The personal statement prompt: Consider a time when someone did something for you that inspired gratitude. How did this experience change you?

8a. First draft

My original home is over the ocean and far away. I grew up in Ukraine, which is a beautiful country, but war has ruined it's landscape and caused fear and despair for the people who live there. Bombing and fighting has killed or wounded many Ukrainians, as well as destroying buildings and artefacts that record Ukraine's history. Lives cannot be replaced, and history is something that once lost, is lost forever.

Many people in Ukraine are against war, but not everyone had the opportunity to escape like me. I was lucky. A group of people in my new country led by [removed identifier] raised money to help my family leave Ukraine. They helped us find a place to live, and gathered donations of furniture, household items, clothing, and other basic necessities. We had left a place without hope but now had optimism for the future. I left the Ukraine as a refugee and was welcomed to a new country and a new life, where I feel safe and can live in dignity.

Part of living in dignity is being able to be part of your community. It's important to understand the language of where you live so that you can fully join the community. Language is the key to successfully living in your new home so that you can interact with other people outside your home, at school, and at work. Not being able to speak the language will isolate you and effect your ability to enjoy life.

[Removed identifier] who led the group that brought my family to Ukraine, also took it upon herself to help my family learn the language so that we could participate in our community. [Removed identifier] came to our house every week to give us English lessons, and she also researched and gave us information about organizations in the community that could help us learn the language.

[Removed identifier] is my role model and I aspire to follow her example. I have become involved in her efforts to support refugees from countries all over the world that are facing oppression and war. I work with [removed identifier] to collect donations, find community resources, and practice English skills.

My experience has taught me that the best way to repay someone for their kindness and to show gratitude is by helping someone else. Getting people to safety and establishing them in a new home is [removed identifier]'s passion, but she cannot do it alone. By contributing to this cause, I not only help other refugees, but I show [removed identifier] and other members of the group who supported my family that their efforts were meaningful in my life.

People who live in a place of war have very little control over their situation and are dependent on others to find a way out. [Removed identifier] and those who work with her give refugees a new chance at life so that they can go on to make a difference in the world too. I will be forever grateful to [removed identifier] and hope that I can one day be a hero to someone else just as she is a hero to me.

8b. Exercise: Can you spot the errors?

Use the space below to write down the errors you have spotted. Make sure you do this before moving on to the next section. Besides identifying grammatical errors, also make note of red flags, issues with structure and flow, and so forth. Take your time and refer to *Chapter III: 7 Common Essay Errors* if necessary.

8c. List of errors

Now let's examine the errors our admissions expert identified. To help you better understand our approach, these errors will be bolded and underlined in the revised draft in the following section.

- *Not concise:* Repetitive language or content should be condensed. A concise essay is easier to read and understand. Further, it increases the available word count, which can be diverted to key points.

- *Lack of connection between ideas:* Some statements can be expanded to better connect different ideas presented by the applicant. Every sentence should reflect the essay prompt, and transition statements will help to join seemingly disparate ideas.

- *Need for elaboration:* The applicant has opportunities to elaborate on some of their ideas. Rather than telling the reader reasons they were grateful or how they extended their gratefulness to others, the applicant should share specific examples to personalize their essay and provide context.

- *Minor punctuation or grammatical errors:* There are minor punctuation and grammatical errors in the content, which will distract the reader from the applicant's response. Further, these errors reduce the professionalism of the essay and suggest that the applicant did not take time to review their essay before finalizing it. Fixing these errors will enhance the reader's overall experience and impression of the essay.

- *Weak conclusion:* The purpose of the conclusion is to summarize the essay's content and leave the reader with a lasting impression. However, the applicant does not directly address the essay prompt in the conclusion. The conclusion should be revised to emphasize the applicant's response to both questions in the prompt.

Note: The passages in which the expert left comments or suggestions for the student to review are underlined and marked using superscript numerals. Use these numerals to reference our expert's comments/suggestions listed below the revised draft.

8d. First revision by a BeMo admissions expert

My original home is over the ocean and far away. I grew up in Ukraine, which is a beautiful country, but war has ruined ~~it's~~ **its**[1] landscape and caused fear and despair for the people who live there. Bombing and fighting has killed or wounded many Ukrainians, as well as destroying buildings and artefacts that record Ukraine's history. **Lives cannot be replaced, and history is something that once lost, is lost forever.**[2]

Many people in Ukraine are against war,[3] but not everyone had the opportunity to escape like me. I was lucky. A group of people in my new country led by [removed identifier] raised money to help my family leave Ukraine. They helped us find a place to live,[4] and gathered donations of furniture, household items, clothing, and other ~~basic~~[5] necessities. We had left a place without hope but now had optimism for the future. I left the Ukraine as a refugee and was welcomed to a new country and a new life, where I feel safe and can live in dignity.

Part of living in dignity is being able to be part of your community.[6] **It's important to understand the language of where you live so that you can fully join the community. Language is the key to successfully living in your new home so that you can interact with other people outside your home, at school, and at work.**[7] Not being able to speak the language will isolate you and ~~effect~~ **affect**[8] your ability to enjoy life.

[Removed identifier] who led the group that brought my family to Ukraine, also took it upon herself to help my family learn the language **so that we could participate in our community**.[9] [Removed identifier] came to our house every week to give us English lessons, and she also researched and gave us information about organizations in the community that could help us learn the language.

[Removed identifier] is my role model and I aspire to follow her example. I have become involved in her efforts to support refugees from countries all over the world that are facing oppression and war.

I work with [removed identifier] to collect donations, find community resources, and practice English skills.[10]

My experience has taught me that the best way to repay someone for their kindness and to show gratitude is by helping someone else. Getting people to safety and establishing them in a new home is [removed identifier]'s passion, but she cannot do it alone. By contributing to this cause, I not only help other refugees, but I show [removed identifier] and other members of the group who supported my family that their efforts were meaningful in my life.

People who live in a place of war have very little control over their situation and are dependent on others to find a way out. [Removed identifier] and those who work with her give refugees a new chance at life so that they can go on to make a difference in the world too. I will be forever grateful to [removed identifier] and hope that I can one day be a hero to someone else just as she is a hero to me.[11]

Word count prior to revision: 525

Word count after revision: 525

Word count limit: 650

Expert's comments/suggestions:

1. Be careful of punctuation errors. Before you finalize your essay, take time to read through the entire essay to look for minor punctuation errors. Additionally, use your word processor's editing tool to identify and correct any errors you may have missed.

2. This statement doesn't transition effectively into the next paragraph. I recommend adding another sentence to connect your first paragraph to the second paragraph.

3. This phrase seems out of place. Consider elaborating upon it or removing it.

4. This comma is unnecessary and can be removed.

5. "Basic" and "necessities" have essentially the same meaning. Remove "basic" to be concise.

6. Good work on your transition here! This statement leads the reader from the ideas of the previous paragraph to this one.

7. There's some repetition in the ideas you present in these two sentences. Condensing these sentences into one sentence will make your essay more concise.

8. Watch for homophone (words that sound the same but have different meanings) as you complete a final review of your essay. These words are typically not flagged by word processing built-in editors or spelling tools.

9. What are some specific interactions that benefited from you learning the language? This information will provide context and demonstrate the urgency of learning these skills to live successfully in your new community.

10. To personalize your essay and increase the reader's engagement, share a particular story of your involvement rather than only listing your contributions.

11. The essay prompt has two parts: describing an experience that has inspired your gratitude, and discussing how it has changed you. Your conclusion doesn't directly address the essay prompt. Your conclusion should be a summary of your essay and address both parts of the essay prompt.

Our expert's overall feedback in the end:

Excellent work on your first draft! To further enhance your essay, there are a few changes you can make.

First, be concise. You have a limited word count, so use every word to your benefit. Avoid repetition, and ensure that every statement adds value to your story and supports your response to the essay prompt.

Second, in answering the essay prompt, focus on successfully connecting ideas and transitioning from one idea to the next. The reader needs the full context for why you have made a statement and how it relates to other statements. Further, the reader should be able to easily connect each statement to how it supports the essay prompt.

Third, summarizing the key points of your essay is your priority in the concluding paragraph. The first draft of your essay approaches but does not directly address either of the questions in the essay prompt. Remind the reader of the experience that resulted in your gratitude and how the experience changed you.

Finally, after completing a thorough review of your essay, be sure to use your word processor's built-in editor and spelling tool to identify and correct errors in punctuation, grammar, and spelling prior to finalizing your essay. The reader will appreciate an error-free essay as it's easier to read and demonstrates your professionalism.

Your essay revisions may change your word count. Ensure that your word count adheres to the limits defined for this essay prompt.

Please work on the areas outlined above and submit another draft for review when you're ready!

Cheers,
BeMo

The following document is a final draft that was the result of multiple revisions with our admissions expert. Typically, there are two to three revisions.

8e. Final draft

My original home is over the ocean and far away. I grew up in Ukraine, which is a beautiful country, but war has ruined its landscape and caused fear and despair for the people who live there. Bombing and fighting has killed or wounded many Ukrainians, as well as destroying buildings and artefacts that record Ukraine's history. Lives cannot be replaced, and history is something that once lost, is lost forever. Although Ukraine will always hold special memories for me, the war meant that my family and I could not continue to live there safely.

My family was fortunate to acquire visitor visas in [removed identifier], and a local group sponsored our relocation while we wait for permanent residency. [Removed identifier], the organizer of this group, and other volunteers found us a place to live and gathered donations of furniture, household items, clothing, and other necessities. Thanks to their generosity and time, my family and I now have optimism for the future. We left the Ukraine as refugees without a home, but [removed identifier] and her group welcomed us to a new country where we feel safe and can live in dignity.

Part of living in dignity is being an active participant in your community, which requires understanding the language. Not being able to speak the language can isolate you and affect your ability to enjoy life, as language is the key to successfully interacting with people outside your home, at school, and at work. [Removed identifier] came to my family's house every week to give us English lessons, and she also researched and gave us information about organizations in the community that could help us learn more advanced English skills. Thanks to [removed identifier]'s kindness, my English skills improved significantly, which allowed me to communicate confidently with my teachers, my peers, and people I encountered in my neighborhood.

[Removed identifier] is my role model and I aspire to follow her example. I have become involved in her efforts to support refugees that are facing oppression and war from countries all over the world. I work with [removed identifier] to collect donations, identify community resources, and practice English skills with these newcomers. I've also been able to assist people from my birth country to navigate their new life, including a mother and daughter from

my hometown. I oriented the daughter to the school we both attend, and I meet with them every Sunday to practice conversational English.

My experience has taught me that the best way to repay someone for their kindness and to show gratitude is by helping someone else. Getting people to safety and establishing them in a new home is [removed identifier]'s passion, but she cannot do it alone. By contributing to this cause, I not only help other refugees, but I show [removed identifier] and other members of the group who supported my family that their efforts were meaningful in my life. Now, I can use my experiences to guide others through the process of settling in a new place, whether by finding resources or practicing language skills with them.

[Removed identifier] and those who volunteer with her give refugees like me a new chance at life, which allows us to go on to make a difference in the world too. I will be forever grateful to [removed identifier] and hope that I can be a hero to someone else just as she is a hero to me. She inspired me to share my knowledge and skills with people from around the world who are displaced and struggling. As refugees, we may not be able to control the circumstances that forced us to leave our countries, but we can come together to create a new home where we are finally safe.

8f. Discussion

This applicant improved their essay by correcting minor punctuation errors, as well as making their essay more concise. They removed repetitive content and content that did not support their message. This gave the applicant extra space in their available word count to expand their essay elsewhere. For example, they added specific details of experiences to personalize their essay and engage the reader. This additional content provides clarity for the reader and eases the transition between ideas.

The conclusion was lacking in the first draft. It did not directly reflect the questions asked in the essay prompt. In the final draft, the conclusion summarizes the key points related to the essay prompt. It has also been updated to include a memorable concluding statement.

The personal statement prompt: What part of your identity is fundamental to your story and without which your application would be incomplete?

9a. First draft

I was always the tall girl in school. This may seem like an advantage, but for me it was a source of embarrassment and self-loathing. I vividly remember picture days at school. I was always placed in the back row beside the teacher, while I longingly watched the other girls placed into the bottom and middle rows. Standing in the back row emphasized how I was different from all the other girls. Although I'm sure that no one else even noticed where I was standing or why, to me it was as though a giant spotlight was aimed at me. I felt awkward throughout the whole ordeal and didn't feel a sense of relief until the class was excused to step down from the benches. Pictures only happened once a year, but gym class was several times a week.

My gym teachers were always eager to have me participate in basketball and track and field as they thought I would be a natural because of my height. Although my track and field skills might have been slightly above average, I was awkward and uncoordinated in basketball. My teachers were always disappointed that their dreams of a star basketball player were not realized. In turn, I was disappointed that my height didn't offer even this advantage to me.

High school was difficult as a tall girl, mostly from the social aspect. I struggled to make friends, probably because I was uncomfortable with myself. Another difficulty for me was navigating social events. I always felt like an outsider, which prevented me from being myself. I really wanted to belong, but to belong I had to participate. If I participated, then it meant that attention was placed on me. I couldn't view myself as separate from my height.

It wasn't until my final year of high school that I finally came to the discovery that my height was not my identity. This realization came about during a biology field trip to a marine station. One of our activities was measuring populations of organisms on a local beach. Although the activity itself was uneventful, we took a different route out of the area then when we arrived. This new route was through a section of thick, unforgiving mud that pulled many of us down to our waists or further. I was stuck as well, but I was surprisingly calm during the situation and was able to guide many of my classmates out of the mud. They, in turn, helped me. This situation was the first time I recall not being concerned about my height and engaged fully in the present moment. I blossomed.

The rest of the trip brought out an entirely new side to me. Instead of shyly retreating to the outskirts of different groups, I joked with my classmates, invited myself into conversations, and generally enjoyed myself. It became clear to me that the only person holding me back from being confident in myself and participating in high school experiences was myself.

Growing up, I always believed that being physically different from others was what distanced me from groups and activities, when it was actually me putting up these barriers. It was a disservice to myself to avoid interactions with others, and it was a disservice to those who were truly interested in getting to know me. Having discovered that my perspective was skewed, I'm now proud of my height. It's part of who I am, but it's not the only part.

9b. Exercise: Can you spot the errors?

Use the space below to write down the errors you have spotted. Make sure you do this before moving on to the next section. Besides identifying grammatical errors, also make note of red flags, issues with structure and flow, and so forth. Take your time and refer to *Chapter III: 7 Common Essay Errors* if necessary.

9c. List of errors

Now let's examine the errors our admissions expert identified. To help you better understand our approach, these errors will be bolded and underlined in the revised draft in the following section.

- *Weak introduction:* The introductory statement is too simplistic and lacks creativity. As the reader's crucial first impression, the applicant should strive to make this sentence unique and memorable.

- *Not concise:* There a few places where the applicant could use more concise wording, which will increase their available word count.

- *Minor spelling, punctuation, and grammatical errors:* The essay contains minor spelling, punctuation, and grammatical errors, which deteriorate from the overall quality of the essay. Although some of these errors might be identified by the applicant's word processing tools, such as their editor and spelling tools, other errors can only be found by a careful reading of the entire essay. This review should include applying parallel structure and rewriting overly long sentences.

- *Poor transitions:* Transition statements near the beginning of the essay can be improved. In particular, the sentence at the end of paragraph one introduces the topic of the next paragraph without any context, which may be confusing to the reader.

- *Need for elaboration:* Some points require elaboration. The applicant occasionally makes statements that are not expanded with examples.

Note: **The passages in which the expert left comments or suggestions for the student to review are underlined and marked using superscript numerals. Use these numerals to reference our expert's comments/suggestions listed below the revised draft.**

9d. First revision by a BeMo admissions expert

<u>I was always the tall girl in school.</u>[1] This may seem like an advantage, but for me it was a source of embarrassment and self-loathing. <u>I vividly remember picture days at school. I was always placed in the back row beside the teacher, while I longingly watched the other girls placed into the bottom and middle rows. Standing in the back row emphasized how I was different from all the other girls. Although I'm sure that no one else even noticed where I was standing or why, to me it was as though a giant spotlight was aimed at me. I felt awkward throughout the whole ordeal and didn't feel a sense of relief until the class was excused to step down from the benches.</u>[2] <u>Pictures only happened once a year, but gym class was several times a week.</u>[3]

<u>My gym teachers were always eager to have me participate in basketball and track and field as they thought I would be a natural because of my height.</u>[4] Although my track and field skills might have been slightly above average, I was awkward and uncoordinated in basketball. My teachers were always disappointed that their dreams of a star basketball player were not realized. In turn, I was disappointed that my height didn't offer even this advantage to me.

High school was difficult as a tall girl, mostly from the social aspect. I struggled to make friends, probably because **I was uncomfortable with myself**.[5] Another difficulty for me was navigating social events. I always felt like an outsider, which prevented me from being myself. I really wanted to belong, but to belong I had to participate. If I participated, then it meant that attention was placed on me. I couldn't view myself as separate from my height.

It wasn't until my final year of high school that I finally came to the discovery that my height was not my identity. This realization came about during a biology field trip to a marine station. One of our activities was measuring populations of organisms on a local beach. Although the activity itself was uneventful, we took a different route out of the area ~~then~~ **than**[6] when we arrived. This new route was through a section of thick, unforgiving mud that pulled many of us down to our waists ~~or further~~.[7] I was stuck as well, but I was surprisingly calm during the situation and was able to guide many of my classmates out of the mud. They, in turn, helped me. This situation was the first time I recall not being concerned about my height~~, and engaged~~ **engaging**[8] fully in the present moment. I blossomed.

The rest of the trip brought out an entirely new side to me. Instead of shyly retreating to the outskirts of different groups, I joked with my classmates, invited myself into conversations, and generally enjoyed myself. It became clear to me that the only person holding me back from being confident in myself and participating in ~~high school~~ **social**[9] experiences was myself.

Growing up, I always believed that being physically different from others was what distanced me from groups and activities, when it was actually me putting up these barriers. It was a disservice to myself to avoid interactions with others, and it was a disservice to those who were truly interested in getting to know me. **Having discovered that my perspective was skewed, I'm now proud of my height.**[10] It's part of who I am, but it's not the only part.

Word count prior to revision: 582

Word count after revision: 576

Word count limit: 650

Expert's comments/suggestions:

1. Your opening statement is the reader's first introduction to you and what they will remember most. Make sure this sentence is exciting. Consider retelling a significant experience, asking a question, or sharing a quotation that's meaningful to you.

2. Use this experience to begin your essay. It's a significant aspect of your story and will be more compelling than your current opening statement.

3. This transition statement is awkward and abrupt. Limit this sentence to the current discussion about picture day. Reserve discussion about gym class to the following paragraph.

4. Separate this sentence into two. It will be easier to read, which will also make your ideas easier to grasp by the reader.

5. It might be worthwhile to expand on this point to provide the reader with context. Show, don't tell.

6. This spelling error may not be identified by your word processor's built-in editor or spelling tool as "then" and "than" are homophones. Be sure to complete a final review of your essay after it's finished to locate these types of minor errors.

7. To protect your word count limit, remove any unnecessary words that don't add meaning to your essay.

8. There are some issues with parallel structure in this sentence. The suggested changes will make this sentence easier to read.

9. Use concise wording. Any unnecessary words you remove will increase your available word count limit to be used elsewhere.

10. The concluding paragraph is a good place to reiterate the lessons you learned about yourself relating to confidence and engaging with others.

Our expert's overall feedback in the end:

This is a great first effort! Thank you for sharing your experiences.

Your picture day experiences described in the first paragraph represent a significant recurring episode in your life. To gain the reader's attention from the start, I recommend moving this description to the beginning of the paragraph to replace the sentence that's currently there. This change will engage your reader and entice them to read on.

The body of your essay has some punctuation, spelling, and grammatical errors. Correcting these issues will make your essay polished and professional. To find these errors, use your word processor's built-in editor and spelling tool. Additionally, complete a full review of your essay before finalizing it. A final review will also help you discover any awkward phrasing, poor transitions, and wording that lacks conciseness.

You can personalize your essay by providing specific examples to back up your statements. For example, instead of stating the way you felt about yourself, explain why. This information is part of your identity, which is the focus of this essay prompt.

Your essay revisions may change your word count. Ensure that your word count adheres to the limits defined for this essay prompt.

Please work on the areas outlined above and submit another draft for review when you're ready!

Cheers,
BeMo

The following document is a final draft that was the result of multiple revisions with our admissions expert. Typically, there are two to three revisions.

9e. Final draft

I vividly remember picture days at school. As the tall girl, I was always placed in the back row beside the teacher, while I longingly watched the other girls placed into the bottom and middle rows. Standing in the back row emphasized my difference from the other girls. Although I'm sure that no one even noticed where I was standing or why, to me it was as though a giant spotlight was aimed at me. I felt awkward throughout the whole ordeal and did not feel a sense of relief until the class was excused from the benches. Luckily, picture day only happened once a year.

Gym class, unfortunately, was scheduled several times a week. My gym teachers were always eager to have me participate in basketball and track and field. They thought I would be a natural at these sports because of my height. Although my track and field skills might have been slightly above average, I was awkward and uncoordinated in basketball. My teachers were always disappointed that their dreams of a star basketball player were not realized. In turn, I was disappointed that my height did not offer even this advantage to me.

High school was difficult as a tall girl, mostly from the social aspect. I struggled to make friends because I was uncomfortable with myself. Since I found fault with myself, it seemed logical to assume that others would find fault with me also. My self-criticism was especially prominent while navigating social events. I always felt like an outsider, which prevented me from being my authentic self. I really wanted to belong, but to belong I had to participate. If I participated, then it meant that attention was placed on me. I could not view myself as separate from my height.

It was not until my final year of high school that I finally came to the discovery that my height was not my identity. This realization came about during a week-long biology field trip to a marine station. One of our activities was measuring populations of organisms on a local beach. Although the activity itself was uneventful, we took a different route out of the area than when we arrived. This new route was through a section of thick, unforgiving mud that pulled many of us down to our waists. I was stuck as well, but I was surprisingly calm during the situation and was able to guide many of my classmates out of the mud. They, in turn, helped me. This situation was the first time I recall not being concerned about my height, engaging fully in the present moment. I blossomed in this environment.

The rest of the trip brought out an entirely new side to me. Instead of shyly retreating to the outskirts of different groups, I joked with my classmates, invited myself into conversations, and generally enjoyed myself. It became clear to me that the only person holding me back from being confident in myself and participating in social experiences was myself.

Growing up, I always believed that being physically different from others was what distanced me from groups and activities, when it was actually me putting up these barriers. It was a disservice to myself to avoid interactions with others, and it was a disservice to those who were truly interested in getting to know me. Having discovered that my perspective was skewed, I am now proud of my height. It is part of who I am, but it is not the only part. I am intelligent, witty, curious, passionate, and strong in equal measure.

9f. Discussion

Small changes can make big impacts on the quality of an essay. In this example, the applicant changed the entire tone of the beginning of the essay simply by reorganizing the content. A bland introductory statement was replaced by a significant experience in the applicant's life, which shaped their identity across repeated occurrences.

The applicant made other small improvements throughout the essay. Punctuation, spelling, and grammatical errors were addressed. Eliminating these errors allows the reader to focus on the essay content instead of minor distractions in the writing. Further, the applicant replaced awkward phrasing, poor transitions, and wording that was not concise.

The final draft of the essay is more personalized. The applicant expanded their statements to provide concrete examples and a relatable context. These changes will certainly lend to a positive reception from the reader.

The personal statement prompt: What advice would you give your younger self about being a successful student?

10a. First draft

Being a student is hard, but it's a necessary journey to become your best version of yourself. When you are young, the world is full of possibilities. As a young child you explore the environment around you, try new things, consider new ideas, and see the world not for what it is, but for what it could be. When you start school, these explorations become more focused as you begin to learn what others have already discovered about math, science, language, and social interactions. You come to appreciate art, music, and physical education as ways to express yourself, but you also learn that these subjects have the potential to be more personally rewarding when they are given a structure.

As I look back on my education, I realize that the parts of school that I disliked the most were actually the things that I can appreciate the most as an adult. Studying for tests, preparing school projects, and giving presentations were activities that I avoided as a child or put off until the last possible moment. Tests were stressful for me because of the pressure of needing to perform well. It wasn't so much that I disliked studying, but I often worried that I was studying the wrong things or that I didn't understand the content as well as I thought. School projects caused similar anxiety; I didn't always know if the topic or content I selected was aligned correctly with what the teacher expected from me. Finally, oral presentations meant that I had to demonstrate my knowledge or lack thereof in front of my peers. If I didn't get something right, it was there for everyone to see. Looking back, I can tell you that these anxieties were more about my feelings about myself than about my feelings about learning.

One lesson that you can only learn from experience is that learning is a process, not a destination. You will spend your entire life learning, whether at school or through simply interacting with the world around you. Instead of approaching learning with fear and intimidation, consider the joy you gain from the journey. Learning contributes to your own personal growth, and the ways in which you apply your learning have impacts on the world around you. As you pursue your career in the social sciences, this means that you will have a direct influence on the lives of the people you work with.

So, how do you change your approach to learning as a student to something more positive? Remove the focus on learning as an outcome. The goal is not to pass the test, ace the project, or wow the class with your amazing presentation skills. Instead, the goal is to achieve value and direction for yourself. What have you learned? How can you use this learning to change the world for yourself and others?

If I could go back in time, I would use the opportunity to go beyond what my teachers assigned. I would research topics I was interested in, experiment with my own projects, and take time to share my knowledge with others. Being a student is one of the most enjoyable and rewarding times of life: take all the advantages you have to learn and to share your learning with others.

10b. Exercise: Can you spot the errors?

Use the space below to write down the errors you have spotted. Make sure you do this before moving on to the next section. Besides identifying grammatical errors, also make note of red flags, issues with structure and flow, and so forth. Take your time and refer to *Chapter III: 7 Common Essay Errors* if necessary.

10c. List of errors

Now let's examine the errors our admissions expert identified. To help you better understand our approach, these errors will be bolded and underlined in the revised draft in the following section.

- *Poor word choice and phrasing:* The applicant occasionally does not use precise wording, which impacts the clarity of their essay. Further, there are some phrases that are awkward and would benefit from rewording to make them more concise. In particular, the applicant should remove repetitive wording.

- *Need for elaboration:* There are a couple of instances where the applicant can expand their thoughts to provide the reader with a better understanding of the practical implications of their ideas.

Note: **The passages in which the expert left comments or suggestions for the student to review are underlined and marked using superscript numerals. Use these numerals to reference our expert's comments/suggestions listed below the revised draft.**

10d. First revision by a BeMo admissions expert

Being a student is hard, but it's a necessary **part of the**[1] journey to become your best version of yourself. When you are young, the world is full of possibilities. As a ~~young~~[2] child,[3] you explore the environment around you, try new things, consider new ideas, and ~~see~~ **envision**[4] the world not for what it is, but for what it could be. When you start school, these explorations become more focused as you begin to learn what others have already discovered about math, science, language, and social interactions. You come to appreciate art, music, and physical education as ways to express yourself~~, but you~~ **You**[5] also learn that these subjects have the potential to be more personally rewarding when they are given a structure.

As I look back on my education, I realize that the parts of school that I disliked the most were ~~actually~~[6] the things that I can appreciate the most as an adult. **Studying for tests, preparing school projects, and giving presentations were activities that I avoided as a child or put off until the last possible moment.**[7] Tests were stressful for me because of the pressure of needing to perform well. It wasn't so much that I disliked studying, but I often worried that I was studying the wrong things or that I didn't understand the content as well as I thought. School projects caused similar anxiety; I didn't always know if the topic or content I selected was aligned correctly with what the teacher expected from me. Finally, oral presentations meant that I had to demonstrate my knowledge or lack thereof in front of my peers. If I didn't get something right, it was there for everyone to see. Looking back, ~~I can tell you that~~[8] these anxieties were more about my feelings ~~about~~ **toward**[9] myself than about my feelings ~~about~~ **toward**[10] learning.

One lesson that you can only learn from experience is that learning is a process, not a destination. You will spend your entire life learning, whether at school or through **simply interacting with the world around you.**[11] Instead of approaching learning with fear and intimidation, consider the joy you gain from the journey. Learning contributes to your own personal growth, and the ways in which you apply your learning have impacts on the world around you. As you pursue your career in the social sciences, this means that you will have a direct influence on the lives of the people you work with.

So, how do you change your approach to learning ~~as a student~~[12] to something more positive? Remove the focus on learning as an outcome. The goal is not to pass the test, ace the project, or wow the class with your amazing presentation skills. Instead, the goal is to achieve value and direction for yourself. What have you **learned**?[13] How can you use this learning to change the world for yourself and others?

If I could go back in time, I would use the opportunity to go beyond what my teachers assigned. I would research topics I was interested in, experiment with my own projects, and take time to share my knowledge with others. Being a student is one of the most enjoyable and rewarding times of life: take ~~all the advantages you have to learn~~ **every chance you have to learn**[14] and to share your learning with others.

Word count prior to revision: 547

Word count after revision: 538

Word count limit: 650

Expert's comments/suggestions:

1. To be more precise, this sentence should refer to your time as a student as a part of your journey, not the whole journey.

2. You can remove this word as it's redundant. A child is young by definition.

3. Add a comma here to break up your sentence into easy-to-read phrases.

4. "Envision" is a less common and more powerful word. A thesaurus is a great tool to use while you're writing essays. A thesaurus can give you ideas to increase your word variety.

5. This phrase should be presented as a separate sentence. It refers to the prior two sentences, so separating it will ensure that your meaning is not misunderstood.

6. Removing unnecessary words will improve your essay's conciseness. Further, it will give you additional words to use more effectively elsewhere since you have a word count limit.

7. It can be tempting to list things without expanding on them further. You've done an excellent job of explaining each of the things you mention in this list as part of the rest of your paragraph.

8. Although the essay prompt directs you to speak to your younger self, the wording you've used here is cluttered and unnecessary. Remove this phrase to be more concise.

9. This sentence uses the word "about' on four occasions, which is repetitive and distracts from your idea. Replacing two of these instances with "toward" will improve this sentence greatly.

10. This instance of "about" should also be replaced with "toward."

11. Earlier in the essay, you discussed ways you learn at school (e.g., through taking exams, preparing projects, and giving presentations). Can you expand on what you view as learning through interacting with the world around you?

12. You established earlier in the essay that learning can also occur outside of school through daily interactions. Therefore, this phrase is not accurate.

13. Expand on this statement. The discussion is already about learning in general. In this statement, you should be narrowing your ideas into specifics. For example, "What have you learned that you can apply elsewhere?"

14. This phrase is awkward and can be improved by minor changes to wording.

Our expert's overall feedback in the end:

Congratulations on completing your first draft! You have a great foundation for your essay submission.

Two areas you should work on for subsequent drafts are your phrasing and expanding your ideas. In terms of phrasing, be sure to use precise and concise wording. The reader needs to be able to review your essay quickly without struggling to understand your meaning. Remove awkward phrasing and repetitive wording. In terms of elaboration, there are a couple of instances noted in the feedback where you can expand on your thoughts. Don't only explain concepts; explain the practical implications of those concepts.

Your essay revisions may change your word count. Ensure that your word count adheres to the limits defined for this essay prompt.

Please work on the areas outlined above and submit another draft for review when you're ready!

Cheers,
BeMo

The following document is a final draft that was the result of multiple revisions with our admissions expert. Typically, there are two to three revisions.

10e. Final draft

Being a student is hard, but it is a necessary part of the journey to become your best version of yourself. When you are young, the world is full of possibilities. As a child, you explore the environment around you, try new things, consider new ideas, and envision the world not for what it is, but for what it could be. When you start school, these explorations become more focused as you begin to learn what others have already discovered about math, science, language, and social interactions. You come to appreciate art, music, and physical education as ways to express yourself. You also learn that these subjects have the potential to be more personally rewarding when they are given a structure.

As I look back on my education, I realize that the parts of school that I disliked the most were the things that I can appreciate the most as an adult. Studying for tests, preparing school projects, and giving presentations were activities that I avoided as a child or delayed until the last possible moment. Tests were stressful for me because of the pressure of needing to perform well. It was not so much that I disliked studying, but I often worried that I was studying the wrong things or that I did not understand the content as well as I thought. School projects caused similar anxiety; I did not always know if the topic or content I selected was aligned correctly with what the teacher expected from me. Finally, oral presentations meant that I had to demonstrate my knowledge or lack thereof in front of my peers. If I did not get something right, it was there for everyone to see. Looking back, these anxieties were more about my feelings toward myself than about my feelings toward learning.

One lesson that you can only learn from experience is that learning is a process, not a destination. You will spend your entire life learning, whether at school or through simply interacting with the world around you. Outside of a school environment, you will encounter and learn from people of different ages, interact in business environments, navigate unstructured situations, and encounter the natural world. Instead of approaching learning with fear and intimidation, consider the joy you gain from the journey. Learning contributes to your own personal growth, and the ways in which you apply your learning have impacts on the world around you. As you pursue your career in the social sciences, this means that you will have a direct influence on the lives of the people you work with.

So, how do you change your approach to learning to something more positive? Remove the focus on learning as an outcome. The goal is not to pass the test, ace the project, or wow the class with your amazing presentation skills. Instead, the goal is to achieve value and direction for yourself. What have you learned that you can apply elsewhere? How can you use this learning to change the world for yourself and others?

If I could go back in time, I would use the opportunity to go beyond what my teachers assigned. I would research topics I was interested in, experiment with my own projects, and take time to share my knowledge with others. Being a student is one of the most enjoyable and rewarding times of life: take every chance you have to learn and to share your learning with others.

10f. Discussion

The applicant's first draft was already well done. They followed the recommendations to refine their essay and increase the overall quality. These recommendations included improving their phrasing and expanding their ideas. They used more precise and concise wording to support their intended meaning. With respect to elaborating on the original content, they provided practical examples to explain concepts.

Summary

Big edits, small edits, *everything* matters! Now that you have had an opportunity to go over 10 personal statements reviewed by our admissions experts, you should have a better understanding of what the process looks like, and all the work that goes into creating a powerful essay. More importantly, you should know the common errors to avoid so you can ensure an efficient process. However, keep in mind you do not want to compromise quality, which is why you need to set out with a game plan.

Remember, when you approach your personal statement, you want to ensure that you are genuine when discussing the experiences that have shaped you and your passions. Consider the amount of time it will take to weave those experiences together into a meaningful story, and also the time you will need in between revisions to improve your essay. Ideally, you want to complete your personal statement before the application systems open, so work backwards to see when you should begin. For some, one month of full commitment to the essay is sufficient, while for others, the process may take longer. The personal statement is not something you want to write again, so give it all that you have.

To see progress, you need to be open to constructive feedback and be willing to work on areas that require modifications and restructuring. Of course, our purpose is only to guide you toward an effective way of telling your story, but discretion is yours on how you want it to be conveyed. When we reviewed the before and after of the 10 personal statements, you may have noticed that on a few occasions, there were one or two minor suggestions that were not implemented in the final draft because the applicants preferred that way of expressing their ideas. This is okay, so as long as the writing is well-structured, grammatical, and doesn't hinder the reader from understanding your message. After all, the personal statement is your own story for your Ivy League application.

In the next chapter, you will have the chance to see the revision process of 8 supplemental essays.

Get ready to take more notes!

CHAPTER V

8 Supplemental Essay Examples

As mentioned in *Chapter I: Why Do We Write Personal Statements?*, after you have diligently completed your personal statement, you may have yet another crucial opportunity to showcase your experiences and values in supplemental essays, such as college-specific essays or written supplements.

Through these additional essays, the admissions committee will want to get to know you better by asking you more about some areas that were not specifically covered in the personal statement. They will usually ask questions that are specific to their own institution to assess how well your experiences and values align with their school's goals and philosophies. Essentially, they want to see if you will be a good fit for their school. Supplemental essays are a very important part of the application process and should not be taken lightly. The number and length of the essays required vary by school.

So, what additional information do Ivy League schools want to know from you? While they are allowed to ask applicants anything within reason, many Ivy League schools are interested in knowing similar types of information about their applicants. Similar to the personal statement, the following topics commonly appear in supplemental essay prompts:

- Your reasons for choosing our school

- Your cultural competency

- Overcoming challenges

- Your future goals

- Explanation of academic lapse or breaks

These topics were intentionally made vague so they can be applicable to all essay prompts. Oftentimes, some of these topics can overlap. For more details, refer to *Chapter I: Why Do We Write Personal Statements?*. Regardless of the essay prompt, the principles that were discussed for writing a strong personal statement, such as *show, not tell,* apply to supplemental essays as well. Since these essays have strict word limits, it is especially important to be concise and to the point. If necessary, review the principles discussed in the previous chapters before proceeding to make the most of this chapter.

Like *Chapter IV: 10 Personal Statement Examples: From First Draft to Acceptance-Magnet Final Draft*, which reviewed 10 personal statements, this chapter will go through supplemental essays from past BeMo students. Again, you will be able to see the process from beginning to end. For the essays included, we removed personal identifiers for the students' confidentiality.

To review the process again, we will cover the following:

a. <u>First draft</u>: The exact copy sent in by a student for a BeMo review.

b. <u>Exercise</u>: Your opportunity to list the errors you find throughout the essay. Pay close attention to not only grammatical errors, but also to structural and organizational issues.

c. <u>List of errors</u>: A list of errors our admissions expert has identified and explanations of what the student should and should not do.

d. <u>First revision by an expert</u>: The first review by one of our admissions experts, including revisions and comments.

e. <u>Final draft</u>: The final draft after the student has considered our feedback and made revisions based on our suggestions.

f. <u>Discussion</u>: An overview of the changes that were made and a discussion of how the applicants were able to alter their personal statements to completely transform them into acceptance magnets!

As we go through each stage of improving these essays, take notes and refer back to the previous chapters if necessary to work through the exercise.

Are you ready? Here we go again!

The supplemental essay prompt: What would you say is your greatest talent or skill? How have you developed and demonstrated that talent over time? (250-word limit)

1a. First draft

The best talent I have developed so far is the ability to speak in five different languages. I always had a passion to learn different languages since my childhood. During high school, I joined the language club where I learned Japanese and Cantonese. As Fellini once said, "A different language is a different vision of life." I truly believe in this quote, because as I began learning different languages, it opened up my vision, and my perspective toward life. With this talent, I believe it will strongly help me in communicating effectively throughout my professional career.

1b. Exercise: Can you spot the errors?

Use the space below to write down the errors you have spotted. Make sure you do this before moving on to the next section. Besides identifying grammatical errors, also make note of red flags, issues with structure and flow, and so forth. Take your time and refer to *Chapter III: 7 Common Essay Errors* if necessary.

1c. List of errors

Now let's examine the errors our admissions expert identified. To help you better understand our approach, these errors will be bolded and underlined in the revised draft in the following section.

- *Telling rather than showing:* The applicant needs to show, by providing an example, rather than just stating or telling (for example, how learning different languages expanded the applicant's vision). Due to word constraints, a short example is sufficient to include.

- *Ineffective transition:* It is not recommended to write different paragraphs for a short, limited word essay; however, the small paragraph should have a clear introduction, body, and conclusion. The applicant's essay lacks this transition.

- *Examples need expansion:* The applicant should justify the written statements by backing them up with sound examples. For example, in the conclusion, merely writing that different languages will help in their professional career is not enough. A reason for this should be provided.

- *Poor conclusion:* The conclusion seems to be missing something, with simply a statement provided at the end. An example of how or where the applicant can effectively communicate will strengthen the conclusion.

Note: **The passages in which the expert left comments or suggestions for the student to review are underlined and marked using superscript numerals. Use these numerals to reference our expert's comments/suggestions listed below the revised draft.**

1d. First revision by a BeMo admissions expert

The best talent I have developed so far is the ability to speak in five different languages. I always had a passion to learn different languages since my childhood. During high school, I joined the language club where I learnt **Japanese and Cantonese.**[1] As Fellini once said, **"A different language is a different vision of life."**[2] I truly believe in this quote, because as I began learning different languages, **it opened up my vision, and my perspective toward life.**[3] **With this talent, I believe it will strongly help me in communicating effectively throughout my professional career.**[4]

Word count prior to revision: 96

Word count after revision: 96

Word count limit: 250

Expert's comments/suggestions:

1. Only two languages are mentioned in the essay. Because five languages are not too many to be listed, you should include the names of all five languages to increase the weight of your application. You can also mention in a hierarchy when and where you learned the different languages.

2. This is good quote, and it makes the essay strong. However, it should either come as an introduction, or right after the first sentence. Putting the quote in the middle brings about an uneven transition.

3. How? You are merely stating and not providing any examples as to how this opened up your vision. A short example here will make the essay strong.

4. Why do you believe that speaking different languages will be an added help and a great incentive in your career? The school will want to learn more about how this talent can

benefit you on a long-term basis with respect to your professional field. This also makes the conclusion vague, leaving the whole essay not as strong as it should be.

Our expert's overall feedback in the end:

Your response to the essay prompt lacks sound examples and mostly states, rather than depicts or shows. There is a lack of transition between different sentences, while the focus is mostly on learning languages, rather than on how the learned languages will be implemented or will be beneficial in the future. Additionally, the prompt also asks you to identify how you have demonstrated your talent over time, something which is entirely missing from this essay. In general, try to focus on what the prompt is asking and provide significant examples to back up any statements. You still have a substantial amount of space to elaborate on the examples considering the essay is only 97 words, whereas the limit is 250 words.

The following document is a final draft that was the result of multiple revisions with our admissions expert. Typically, there are two to three revisions.

1e. Final draft

Fellini once said, "A different language is a different vision of life." The best talent I have developed so far is the ability to speak in five different languages. I realized my passion for learning various languages when I was 5 years old. Initially, I began to speak and write English as my native language, after which I was introduced to Spanish as a secondary language at school. During high school, I joined the language club where I learned Japanese and Cantonese. I was always fascinated by the Far Eastern culture, and learning their language proved to be a stepping stone during my voluntary internship at a medical camp in China. As I began to learn different languages, I realized that it opened my vision and my perspective toward life. I began realizing the gap in communication, which the world faces today, is prominently due to language barriers. Currently, I am learning Persian due to its link with ancient medicine in Mesopotamia. I do not plan to stop here. I strongly believe that the ability to communicate in different languages will help me in my professional career, especially during those instances where I will have to treat patients from different cultures and ethnic backgrounds. An effective communication medium will establish a strong relationship between the patient and myself. With this notion, I plan to continue learning different languages of interest, with the next one being Arabic.

1f. Discussion

The essay prompt asks the applicant to discuss the greatest talent that they have developed over time and how they have demonstrated that talent until now. The first draft submitted by the applicant was lacking in several aspects. It contained incoherent transitions between sentences, lack of sound examples, and vague statements. There was scope for improvement, which the applicant worked upon subsequently, and in the end, they were able to finally draft a clear, simple, yet effective essay of 239 words compared to the initial 97 words.

In the first draft, the applicant did not state all the languages they had learned, which is the focus of this essay. Linking those languages to how they helped the applicant during their life, and their reason for learning those languages, was also something that was lacking in the first draft. This was ultimately developed into a more coherent form in the end.

The supplemental essay prompt: Describe your leadership style. Provide a specific example of how you have applied your leadership style. (250-word limit)

2a. First draft

I think I have a democratic leadership style. The reason I would assume this is because I love to work in a team and encourage other team member's opinions. During a course project for a chemistry class in high school, I was made the team head by my teacher. The requirement was to finish a case study analysis requiring the group to critically analyze on the experimental setups of some chemical reactions. This required a final decision in the end, whether the setup given was perfect or could be modified to be made better. During this time, I involved all my team members, and took their opinions on the setup, and in the end submitted a combined report based on a mutual decision, rather than only what I thought. I believe my democratic style of leadership can be beneficial in the long run, especially during my career, where I can welcome colleagues' opinions on a project, or even during team discussions and projects during academic courses.

2b. Exercise: Can you spot the errors?

Use the space below to write down the errors you have spotted. Make sure you do this before moving on to the next section. Besides identifying grammatical errors, also make note of red flags, issues with structure and flow, and so forth. Take your time and refer to *Chapter III: 7 Common Essay Errors* if necessary.

2c. List of errors

Now let's examine the errors our admissions expert identified. To help you better understand our approach, these errors will be bolded and underlined in the revised draft in the following section.

- *Weak introduction:* The applicant needs to show confidence in their leadership style. Starting with "I think" demonstrates a lack of confidence and that the applicant is unsure of their own leadership style.

- *Poor word choice:* Sentences should have a variety of words to demonstrate a sound vocabulary. The applicant has used the word "requirement" or "required" several times in the same sentence.

- *Poor structure:* The applicant successfully conveys the example linked with their leadership style; however, sentence formation can be improved for a more professional tone.

- *Poor conclusion:* The concluding sentence can be rewritten with better grammar, punctuation, and conciseness. Presently, it has three lines, which can be broken down for better coherency.

Note: **The passages in which the expert left comments or suggestions for the student to review are underlined and marked using superscript numerals. Use these numerals to reference our expert's comments/suggestions listed below the revised draft.**

2d. First revision by a BeMo admissions expert

I **think**[1] I have a democratic leadership style. The reason **I would assume**[2] this is because I love to **work in a team**[3] and encourage other team member's opinions. **During a chemistry course project** ~~course project for a chemistry class~~ in high school, I was made the team ~~head~~ **leader** by my teacher. The **requirement**[4] was to finish a case study ~~analysis requiring the group to~~ **where we had to** critically analyze ~~on~~ the experimental setups of ~~some~~ **various** chemical reactions. **In the end, a collective report was to be submitted suggesting whether the given setup** ~~This required a final decision in the end, whether the setup given~~ was perfect or ~~could be~~ **required modifications.** ~~modified to be made better.~~ During this time, I involved all my team members, and took their opinions on the setup, **and in** the end submitted a combined report based on a mutual decision, rather than only what I thought. I believe my democratic style of leadership can be beneficial in the long run **of my career.** ~~especially during my career, where~~ Through this approach, I ~~can~~ **will always** welcome **opinions from colleagues, and try to reach conclusions through effective discussions and mutual opinions.** ~~colleagues' opinions on a project, or even during team discussions and projects during academic courses.~~

Word count prior to revision: 166

Word count after revision: 167

Word count limit: 250

Expert's comments/suggestions:

1. The prompt asks about your leadership style. In this instance, you should be firm in your opinion. The word "think" here reflects that you are unsure of your style.

2. This again depicts uncertainty, and words like "assumed" should be avoided in such instances. Instead, use affirmative phrases such as "I believe" or "I have."

3. Enjoyment of teamwork does not necessarily signify democratic leadership qualities. It merely reflects teamwork capability.

4. Avoid word repetition to demonstrate a wider vocabulary. Repetition is redundant and usually makes the reader lose interest in your essay.

Our expert's overall feedback in the end:

Your response to the essay prompt is easy to understand. However, it can be rewritten with better vocabulary by avoiding repetitive words. A sound, integral essay is essential, and confusing phrases such as "I think" or "I assume" make the reader wonder whether you are certain or uncertain of what you are writing. You need to work on sentence formation and sentence structuring. There is still plenty of room for improvement and elaboration considering the essay word limit is 250 words, and the current essay is just 168 words.

The following document is a final draft that was the result of multiple revisions with our admissions expert. Typically, there are two to three revisions.

2e. Final draft

My style of leadership is democratic. Instead of an autocratic approach, I like to consider the opinions of others as I work. I realized this during a chemistry project, where I was made the team leader of my group. The requirement of the project was to critically analyze the experimental setups of various chemical reactions. In the end, a collective report was to be submitted analyzing the applicability of the setups and if any modifications were necessary. To complete this project, I suggested that my team members first study the experiments on their own. After that, we all met and exchanged our ideas to spot any concerns that could cause problems during the reactions. We all noted down our points on pieces of paper, which were consequently shared with each other. All the points were incorporated into the final report, demonstrating that all suggestions were welcomed and were equally important. I believe my democratic style of leadership will be beneficial in the long run of my career. Through this approach, I will always appreciate and welcome opinions from my colleagues and try to reach mutual agreement on complex issues through effective discussions.

2f. Discussion

The essay prompt asks the applicant about their leadership style and how they may have applied it during a specific time. The applicant tries their best to convey the important points; however, the essay lacks coherency and proper sentence formation. The use of repetitive words, as well as ambiguous words, should be avoided whenever writing an essay.

After several revisions, the applicant successfully drafted a coherent, concise, yet clear essay addressing their leadership style. The example of the chemistry class group project was not elaborated in the first draft, while the final draft contains more information as to how the applicant demonstrated their leadership style.

The supplemental essay prompt: Describe your personal experience in community service, volunteer work, or service/help to another. What did you learn from this experience? (200-word limit)

3a. First draft

During my last year of high school summer vacation, I pursued a voluntary service at the old age home. During that time, I learned several aspects of the old age home, including how they function, the medical care they provide, and basic assistances. During this time, I became friends with an old couple with whom I enjoyed watching sports, reading, and listening to music. I used to go there every Tuesday for atleast 3 hours. That was the best volunteer work I had taken for a while, as it taught me compassion, patience, and sense of purpose.

3b. Exercise: Can you spot the errors?

Use the space below to write down the errors you have spotted. Make sure you do this before moving on to the next section. Besides identifying grammatical errors, also make note of red flags, issues with structure and flow, and so forth. Take your time and refer to *Chapter III: 7 Common Essay Errors* if necessary.

3c. List of errors

Now let's examine the errors our admissions expert identified. To help you better understand our approach, these errors will be bolded and underlined in the revised draft in the following section.

- *Poor word choice:* The applicant needs to show more variety in their vocabulary. On several occasions, a sentence is started with the same set of words, thus reflecting poor writing.

- *Punctuation and grammar errors:* It is highly recommended to re-read an essay out loud after writing. Reading your essay several times helps in identifying any grammatical mistakes.

- *Need for elaboration:* The applicant could have elaborated on the voluntary outcomes. This seems lacking in the essay.

- *Poor conclusion:* The conclusion is written poorly. The conclusion needs revision to incorporate a more effective stance on the community service outcome.

- *Inconsistency:* Several sentences lack connection and jump suddenly from one point to another.

- *Too short:* The essay is very short. The word limit is 200 words, and the essay is not even half of the limit. The essay can be expanded further to include and elaborate on several aspects of the service the applicant undertook.

<u>Note</u>: **The passages in which the expert left comments or suggestions for the student to review are underlined and marked using superscript numerals. Use these numerals to reference our expert's comments/suggestions listed below the revised draft.**

3d. First revision by a BeMo admissions expert

During my last year of high school summer vacation, I pursued a voluntary service **at the old age home.**[1] During that time, I learned several aspects of the **old age home,**[2] including how they function, the medical care they provide, and basic <u>assistances</u> **services they offer. During**[3] this time, I became friends with an old couple with whom I enjoyed watching sports, reading, and listening to music. I used to go there every Tuesday for ~~atleast~~ **at least 3 three hours.**[4] That was the best volunteer work I had taken for a while, **as it taught me compassion, patience, and sense of purpose.**[5]

Word count prior to revision: 97

Word count after revision: 98

Word count limit: 200

Expert's comments/suggestions:

1. The correct grammar is "at an old age home." Be careful with grammar and punctuation.

2. "Old age home" has already been mentioned in the first sentence. Try to avoid repetition.

3. A variety in starting words will add more flavor to the essay. The second sentence already starts with 'During.' Thus, another word should be used to start the third sentence.

4. In this sentence, you mention the duration of the voluntary work. This sentence is unrelated to the surrounding content and can be better incorporated at the beginning.

5. Reflect and include more points, and elaborate, if possible, on the things you learned during your experience at the old age home.

Our expert's overall feedback in the end:

Your introduction is good and concise. However, avoid using repetitive words and reflect on the valuable lessons you learned from the voluntary service you pursued. A personal reflection will add more weight to the essay. In your first draft, you are merely stating rather than demonstrating. For example, you could elaborate on how you benefited by watching TV or listening to music with the couple. There is room for improvement by expanding on several points as the essay limit is 200 words, and the first draft is only 97 words.

The following document is a final draft that was the result of multiple revisions with our admissions expert. Typically, there are two to three revisions.

3e. Final draft

During my last year of high school, I pursued a voluntary service at an old age home. I used to go there every Tuesday morning for at least three hours. I had always wanted to spend time with the elderly community, and my summer vacation was the best opportunity to do so. My time at the old age home was well spent. I befriended a couple with whom I used to listen to music, read novels, and watch sports. These activities helped me in understanding my inner strengths and interests. For example, I realized my passion for basketball and football during that time. This community service also helped me learn several aspects of administrative work. It enlightened me about how old age homes function, the medical care they provide, and how they help their members by providing basic services. By far, that was one of my best summers. The time I spent there not only taught me compassion and patience, but also made me realize how important it is for us to celebrate and enjoy the different phases in our lives.

3f. Discussion

The essay prompt asks the applicant to describe an experience of community service or voluntary work. It further asks the applicant to address what they learned from that experience. The first draft submitted by the applicant tackled the prompt quite nicely, addressing the service they chose and some things that they learned from that service. However, the first draft was very short, not even reaching half of the essay word limit. The applicant had merely stated their important points rather than elaborating on them. For example, the applicant stated that they enjoyed listening to music and watching sports with the elderly couple but failed to mention if they learned anything from it.

There was scope for improvement, which the applicant worked on subsequently. In the end, the applicant was able to draft a coherent essay of 181 words compared to the initial 97 words.

The supplemental essay prompt: Briefly elaborate on an activity, organization, work experience, or hobby that has been particularly meaningful to you. (200-word limit)

4a. First draft

One hobby that has been quite meaningful to me is swimming. I used to watch my brother go for swimming each weekend. He always used to return in a good mood and talk about how the sport keeps him fit. Eventually, my mom decided to put me in swimming lessons as well. Initially I struggled, but eventually quickly learned its different forms. Since then, swimming has become my hobby. I now go regularly and there has not been a single weekend for a long time when I have missed my swimming sessions. There were also times when I used to go swimming during the weekdays as well. The sport has instilled new passion in me, keeping me fit, physically as we mentally. I feel swimming has become an integral part of my life which given me that boost to move forward with every day activities. I believe it a great sport to learn and is one of those few one's which utilizes several muscles in the body all at once.

4b. Exercise: Can you spot the errors?

Use the space below to write down the errors you have spotted. Make sure you do this before moving on to the next section. Besides identifying grammatical errors, also make note of red flags, issues with structure and flow, and so forth. Take your time and refer to *Chapter III: 7 Common Essay Errors* if necessary.

4c. List of errors

Now let's examine the errors our admissions expert identified. To help you better understand our approach, these errors will be bolded and underlined in the revised draft in the following section.

- *Poor word choice:* The applicant is encouraged not repeat the essay prompt in the introduction lines. The applicant mentions their brother's good mood due to swimming; however, it is more appropriate here if the applicant focuses on how swimming changes the applicant's own mood rather than their brother's.

- *Poor conclusion:* The conclusion delivers an abrupt ending. A more coherent essay can be written with a fluent transition leading to an obvious yet effective conclusion.

- *Main ideas not introduced:* The applicant talks more about how they got involved in swimming rather than focusing on what they personally achieved from it.

Note: The passages in which the expert left comments or suggestions for the student to review are underlined and marked using superscript numerals. Use these numerals to reference our expert's comments/suggestions listed below the revised draft.

4d. First revision by a BeMo admissions expert

<u>One hobby that has been quite meaningful to me is swimming.</u>[1] <u>I used to watch my brother go for swimming each weekend.</u>[2] <u>He always used to return in a good mood</u>[3] and talk about how the sport keeps him fit. Eventually, my mom decided to put me in swimming lessons as well. After struggling initially, I quickly picked up the different forms of swimming. ~~Initially I struggled, but eventually quickly learned its different forms~~. Since then, swimming has become my hobby. I now go regularly and there has not been a single weekend for a long time when I have missed my swimming sessions. **There were also times when I used to go swimming during the weekdays as well.**[4] The sport has instilled new passion in me, keeping me fit, physically as ~~we~~ **well as** mentally. I feel swimming has become an integral part of my life**,** which has ~~given me that boost to move forward with every day activities~~ **provided me with that boost necessary to carry out daily activities.** <u>I believe it a great sport to learn and is one of</u> ~~those~~ **the few** ~~one's which utilizes~~ **that use several muscles in the body all at once.**[5]

Word count prior to revision: 170

Word count after revision: 173

Word count limit: 200

Expert's comments/suggestions:

1. It is advised not to start the essay by repeating the essay prompt. Provide a unique and compelling introductory line instead.

2. This a mundane sentence and can be rewritten to sound more effective.

3. The purpose of the essay is to share your story. Make sure that the focus more is on you rather than others.

4. Avoid repeating how you frequently went swimming. Instead, use this extra space for elaborating other important points. For example, focus on the meaningful impact of swimming.

5. Though you try to conclude on a positive note, the conclusion can be concisely focused on how swimming benefits you and might help you in your career.

Our expert's overall feedback in the end:

Your introduction is good and concise. However, you should avoid using repetitive words and reflect more on the outcomes of the activity you have mentioned. The essay focuses more on the frequency and your reasons for choosing this activity. The essay is below the word count limit; therefore, use this opportunity to write more about the useful aspects of this activity.

The following document is a final draft that was the result of multiple revisions with our admissions expert. Typically, there are two to three revisions.

4e. Final draft

I always had a passion for swimming. From an early age, I loved the water and was fascinated by the different techniques of this sport. I took inspiration from my brother, who was quite dedicated in his weekly swimming lessons. Eventually, I joined those lessons as well. Initially, despite my enthusiasm, I struggled with the techniques as I had not previously participated in swimming lessons or had someone to instruct me. Nevertheless, with practice, I mastered the sport. Since then, swimming has become my hobby. I regularly swim and try not to miss any sessions with my instructor. Usually, the best time for me to go swimming is on the weekends, allowing me to decompress after a busy week. The sport has instilled a new passion in me, keeping me physically and mentally fit. It has now become an integral part of my routine and necessary to provide that boost to carry out my daily activities. It is one of the few sports that engages almost all the body's muscles. It soothes my nerves and provides me with an opportunity to reflect on complex issues with a fresh mind: something which will help me throughout my personal and professional life.

4f. Discussion

The essay prompt asks the applicant to elaborate on an activity or hobby that they enjoy and that is meaningful to them. The applicant approached the essay prompt quite effectively by being straightforward in their approach. They describe their experiences learning how to swim, which they eventually incorporated as regular activity in their schedule.

The first draft mentioned several of the important aspects of this sport for the applicant, highlighting how they became interested in it and how swimming helps them. However, the prompt asks how the activity has been meaningful in the applicant's life. This discussion was lacking in the first draft.

After much work and effort, the final draft addresses the prompt in a much more coherent way, focusing on the meaningfulness of the sport. Also, the first draft was 170 words, while the final draft is 200 words. Thus, the applicant took advantage of the available word count and elaborated on the many important points of the prompt.

The supplemental essay prompt: Describe an experience or situation that made you feel grateful. (450-word limit)

5a. First draft

There have been many instances in my life which I reflect upon with gratitude, but one in particular stands out. I will always remember an experience I encountered during my solo trip to Turkey. Three years ago, I decided to travel solo. During that trip, something happened which I will always remember. That was my first solo trip. I had partnered with a local home family where I was supposed to stay with them throughout my trip in Istanbul. After landing at the Istanbul airport, I came to know that the family who was supposed to host me could not do so anymore due to a family emergency which required them to fly to another city overnight. Being in a new country where language was a major barrier, this email left me paranoid and worried. I had little money left on me which I had saved for my food expenses, thus booking a hostel or a hotel was out of question. This left me worried. At that time, I had no means to think straight. After clearing the customs, I decided to surf the internet and immediately looked for other options. A Turkish family traveling with me saw my state of worry and asked me about what had happened. Upon listening to me patiently, they offered me help and offered me to stay with them till the original host family returns to Istanbul. After much hesitations, I accepted their kind gesture and decided to move in with them for a few days. They made an amazing host, and I got an opportunity to learn several of Turkish culture and values. I felt extremely thankful to them for this opportunity. They did their best to make me feel at home and introduced me to various Turkish delights. Someday, I hope I will get an opportunity to return this favour to someone else and keep the chain of goodwill going.

5b. Exercise: Can you spot the errors?

Use the space below to write down the errors you have spotted. Make sure you do this before moving on to the next section. Besides identifying grammatical errors, also make note of red flags, issues with structure and flow, and so forth. Take your time and refer to *Chapter III: 7 Common Essay Errors* if necessary.

5c. List of errors

Now let's examine the errors our admissions expert identified. To help you better understand our approach, these errors will be bolded and underlined in the revised draft in the following section.

- *Repetitive:* The applicant repeats several points in the essay. They should use their available word count in a more effective manner. For example, on several occasions, the applicant mentions the word "solo" when describing their trip. The applicant also mentions being "worried" on more than occasion after finding out about their host family's situation.

- *Ineffective transitions:* The applicant moves abruptly from one idea to another, and then returns to the previous idea without transition. A more effective structure is required with fluent transitions to make the essay coherent.

- *Poor word choice:* It is important to re-read the essay after writing it. This will provide the applicant with a chance to identify their own mistakes and can sometimes lead to acknowledging poor word choices. For example, "a local home family" can be replaced by "a local family." Also, sentences that demonstrate a negative or poor thought process in handling difficult situations should be replaced, such as "At that time, I had no means to think straight."

- *Weak sentence structuring:* Several of the sentences are weakly structured. They need to be rewritten with correct grammar and a more professional approach.

Note: The passages in which the expert left comments or suggestions for the student to review are underlined and marked using superscript numerals. Use these numerals to reference our expert's comments/suggestions listed below the revised draft.

5d. First revision by a BeMo admissions expert

There have been many instances in my life ~~which~~ **that I reflect upon with gratitude, but one in particular stands out.**[1] I will always remember an experience I encountered during my solo trip to Turkey. Three years ago, I decided to travel **solo.**[2] During that trip, something happened ~~which~~ **that** I will always remember. That was my first solo **trip.**[3] **I had partnered with a local** ~~home~~ **family** ~~where I~~ **and was supposed to stay with them** ~~throughout~~ **during my** ~~trip~~ **time in Istanbul.**[4] After landing at the Istanbul airport, I came to know that the family who was supposed to host me could not do so anymore due to a family emergency ~~which required them to fly to another city overnight~~. Being in a new country where language was a major barrier, this ~~email~~ **news** left me **paranoid.**[5] ~~and worried~~. I had little money left**,** ~~on me~~ which I had saved for my food expenses, thus booking a hostel or a hotel was out of **the** question. **This left me worried. At that time, I had no means to think straight.**[6] After clearing ~~the~~ customs, **I decided to surf the internet and immediately looked for other options**.[7] A Turkish family traveling with me saw my state of **worry**[8] and asked me about what had happened. Upon listening to me patiently, they offered me help and **offered**[9] **for** me to stay with them ~~till~~ **until** the original host family ~~returns~~ **returned** to Istanbul. ~~After much hesitations,~~ I accepted their kind gesture and decided to move in with them for a few days. They made ~~an~~ amazing ~~host~~ **hosts**, and I got an opportunity to learn ~~several of~~ **about** Turkish culture and values. I felt extremely thankful to them for this opportunity. They did their best to make me feel at home and introduced me to various Turkish delights. **Someday, I hope I will get an opportunity to return this favor to someone else and keep the chain of goodwill going.**[10]

Word count prior to revision: 318

Word count after revision: 301

Word count limit: 450

Expert's comments/suggestions:

1. This is a good beginning sentence.

2. This is repetitive as traveling "solo" has already been mentioned in the second sentence.

3. You have mentioned many times that this was a solo trip. Repeating it will not make it more effective. Avoid repetition where possible.

4. Was it a free stay? Was there something special about it? Elaboration will help, especially since you still have room within your word count limit to write more.

5. This language gives a negative impression of you and suggests that you become overwhelmed easily, which can be detrimental for your application.

6. Avoid using the words "worried," "paranoid," and "petrified." Instead, neutral words should be used that don't reflect an inability to handle tough situations.

7. Good job! This sentence illustrates your traits of resourcefulness and resilience.

8. This word has been repeated several times.

9. It is advised not to use the same words in one sentence to avoid redundancy.

10. This is a good conclusion that shows your commitment to pass on the good deed if and when you have the chance.

Our expert's overall feedback in the end:

You have detailed your story of gratitude nicely. However, there are several instances of repetition and ineffective word choice in your essay. For example, avoid using strong negative words, such as "paranoid" and "worried." These reflect an inability to handle tough situations.

Good structuring is missing from the essay. It is advised to organize the essay into paragraphs, providing the reader with a clear indication of the story flow.

There are several points you can still address in your essay. For example, how did you return the favor to the host family? What valuable lesson did you learn from this experience?

The following document is a final draft that was the result of multiple revisions with our admissions expert. Typically, there are two to three revisions.

5e. Final draft

There are many instances in my life that I often reflect upon with gratitude, but one in particular stands out. I will always remember my experience during my trip to Istanbul, the capital of Turkey.

I am passionate about traveling. Three years ago, after six months of rigorous planning, I decided to travel to Europe, a continent I had not visited before. With a small budget, I found an efficient yet exciting means for my accommodation, which included staying with a local Turkish family. The idea was to experience Turkish culture from its roots, which is more probable if you connect with the locals. After landing at the Istanbul airport, I was planning to take a taxi to the local family's residence, when I learned that the family had an emergency and could no longer offer me a place to stay.

As I was on a limited budget, I did not have enough money to stay at a hotel. Nevertheless, considering this as a great opportunity to learn from unexpected circumstances, I decided to search the internet for possible options. I was hoping to get in touch with a new host family on short notice. To my surprise, a Turkish family at the airport hesitantly approached me to ask if I needed a lift somewhere. I described my situation to them and how I had no other contacts or friends in Istanbul. After listening to me patiently, they offered me help by extending an invitation to stay with them. I was in awe, and this gesture filled me with an abundance of gratitude. My new host family was amazing, and I benefited from the opportunity to learn Turkish culture and values. The family's younger son, who was almost my age, introduced me to various Turkish delights, including local sports and even a popular television series. I never felt a language barrier as we used Google Translate when we could not find the right words. I am extremely thankful to the family for the opportunity they gave me. Helping me when I was completely stranded at the airport, the family offered their home and their time to a stranger.

Leaving the family at the end of my trip was overwhelming. I extended my thanks to each family member and invited them to visit me in Texas where I could host them. I still write to the family, and we often exchange gifts. A good deed goes a long way. Someday, I hope to return this favor to someone else, keeping this chain of goodwill moving with the same zeal and zest that I experienced in Istanbul.

5f. Discussion

The essay prompt asks the applicant to describe an experience that made them grateful. The applicant narrated a story of travel during which they experienced a challenge, yet they were helped by a local family, leaving the applicant full of awe and gratitude.

The first draft of the essay contained repetition, poor sentence structuring, and some ineffective word choices. However, the applicant greatly improved their essay after several revisions. The final draft has proper paragraphs, avoids repetition and negative connotations, and addresses the essay prompt more coherently.

The applicant also added several points to the final essay, bringing the final word count close to the limit of 450 words. In addition, they have expanded on how they felt after the local family's gesture, what they learned from the family, and how they reciprocated. The conclusion ends on a strong note. The applicant shares that they want to keep moving the chain of goodwill forward, which reflects positively on the applicant's personality.

The supplemental essay prompt: What knowledge, skills, and interests will support you in your field of study and as a student of [school]? (400-word limit)

6a. First draft

Carl Sagan once said: "Somewhere, something incredible is waiting to be known". This, for me, captures the essence of science: wondering what we are made of and what can be done with such information. I have been passionate for science since I was little and asked my parents for a microscope for Christmas. I was so interested in everything around me, that I used it to look at my brother's blood, pieces of plants, and insects. I cannot remember a day in which I was not wondering how things happen, how do we walk, talk, and the like.

With genetics courses at school, more questions arose. Because of my fascination for the world of molecular and genetics, I decided to study Biotechnology, with an orientation in Molecular Genetics. I am ever grateful that my parents enabled me to pursue my entire high school in English and become fully fluent, as it has tremendously helped me pursue my scientific aspirations.

I would love to study at [removed identifier], a university that has outstanding resources for scientific research and is in [removed identifier], with all its cultural diversity. I have visited [removed identifier] twice over the years, and [removed identifier] caught my attention, particularly because of its vibrant culture, its diverse population, and openness to cultural diversity. Not surprisingly [removed identifier] is known as the best city for students worldwide. Thus, [removed identifier] seems to be an ideal choice for my further education.

As a final note, over the years I have complemented my studies with social outreach. For instance, I volunteered in non-governmental organizations [removed identifiers], and have become an expert in the communication of Sign Language. I have learned so much helping others and from being in contact with diverse people. This has encouraged me to do social activities related to science, such as being a science tutor for elementary students. These activities helped me grow as a person and I wish to contribute to these values, combined with my passion for science, to my future scientific endeavors.

Thank you very much for your interest and consideration. I tremendously look forward to be given the opportunity to carry out my studies in the [removed identifier] program at [removed identifier], which I would honor to the highest degree.

6b. Exercise: Can you spot the errors?

Use the space below to write down the errors you have spotted. Make sure you do this before moving on to the next section. Besides identifying grammatical errors, also make note of red flags, issues with structure and flow, and so forth. Take your time and refer to *Chapter III: 7 Common Essay Errors* if necessary.

6c. List of errors

Now let's examine the errors our admissions expert identified. To help you better understand our approach, these errors will be bolded and underlined in the revised draft in the following section.

- *Grammatical or spelling errors:* There are instances of missing or incorrect words. The applicant also uses capitalization for many words that do not require it. Unnecessary capitalization makes the writing visually more difficult to read, and it can be distracting.

- *Punctuation errors:* The essay contains minor punctuation errors that will distract the reader. The applicant can identify many of these errors by using their word processor's built-in editor. Any outstanding errors should be captured when the applicant performs a final review of the complete essay.

- *Poor word choice and phrasing:* The applicant occasionally uses incorrect words or phrases, which can be identified by running the word processor's built-in editor and completing a final end-to-end review of the essay.

- *Not concise:* Removing unnecessary words and reducing lengthy phrases will make the essay more concise, polished, and professional.

Note: The passages in which the expert left comments or suggestions for the student to review are underlined and marked using superscript numerals. Use these numerals to reference our expert's comments/suggestions listed below the revised draft.

6d. First revision by a BeMo admissions expert

Carl Sagan once said,[1] **"Somewhere, something incredible is waiting to be known."**[2] **This, for me, captures the essence of science: wondering what we are made of and what can be done with such information.**[3] I have been passionate **about** ~~for~~[4] science since I was **young** ~~little~~[5] and asked my parents for a microscope for Christmas. I was so interested in everything around me,[6] that I used it to look at my brother's blood, pieces of plants, and insects. I cannot remember a day **during** ~~in~~[7] which I was not wondering how things happen, how ~~do~~[8] we walk, **how we**[9] talk, and the like. **With genetics courses at school, more questions arose.**[10] Because of my fascination for the world of molecular ~~and~~[11] genetics, I decided to study **biotechnology**,[12] with an orientation in **molecular genetics**,[13] at [removed identifier] in [removed identifier]. I am ever grateful that my parents enabled me to pursue my entire high school in English and become fully fluent, as it has tremendously helped me pursue my scientific aspirations.

I would love to study at [removed identifier], a university that has outstanding resources for scientific research and is in [removed identifier], with all its cultural diversity. I have visited [removed identifier] twice over the years, and [removed identifier] caught my attention, particularly because of its vibrant culture, its diverse population, and openness to **different cultures** ~~cultural diversity~~.[14] Not surprisingly,[15] [removed identifier] is known as the best city for students worldwide. Thus, [removed identifier] seems to be an ideal choice for my further education.

As a final note, over the years I have complemented my studies with social outreach. For instance, I volunteered in non-governmental organizations [(removed identifiers)],[16] and have become an expert in the communication of **sign language** ~~Sign Language~~.[17] I have learned so much **from**[18] helping others and from being in contact with diverse people. This has encouraged me to **participate in** ~~do~~[19] social activities related to science, such as **tutoring elementary students in science** ~~being a science tutor for elementary students~~.[20] These activities helped me grow as a person. ~~and~~[21] I wish to contribute ~~to~~[22] these values, combined with my passion for science, to my future scientific endeavors.

Thank you very much for your interest and consideration. I tremendously look forward to ~~be given~~[23] the opportunity to carry out my studies in the [removed identifier] program at [removed identifier], which I would honor to the highest degree.

Word count prior to revision: 377

Word count after revision: 378

Word count limit (school specific): 400

Expert's comments/suggestions:

1. Use a comma instead of a colon. Use colons only after an independent clause.

2. Punctuation such as commas and periods should be within rather than outside quotation marks.

3. Excellent work explaining what this quote means to you personally! The admissions committee will appreciate this insight.

4. Be careful with your word choice. Here, "about" and not "for" is the correct word to use.

5. Since this is a formal essay, avoid using colloquial words that you would use in an informal setting.

6. The comma is not required as the phrase that follows is a dependent clause.

7. Be careful with your word choice. Change "in" to "during."

8. When listing items, use parallel structure so that each item in the list is consistent with the other items.

9. This list item also needs to be adjusted to align with the parallel structure of the list.

10. This sentence starts a new thought. Therefore, you should begin a new paragraph. Organizing your essay into appropriate paragraphs allows your reader to clearly distinguish each idea in your essay.

11. There appears to be an extra word here. Before you finalize your essay for submission, review the entire essay to check for this type of error. Minor errors can detract from the professionalism of your essay.

12. Only proper nouns should be capitalized. In this case, the reference is generic and doesn't need to be capitalized.

13. This word is also generic and doesn't need to be capitalized.

14. Watch for repetitive words. A version of "diverse" was used twice in this sentence. To find these types of errors, read through your entire essay before finalizing it.

15. There was a comma missing here.

16. This comma is not required.

17. This term does not need to be capitalized.

18. There was a word missing here. This type of error can be located by reviewing your essay in full before submitting it.

19. Replace casual language with formal language appropriate to an essay format.

20. Your original statement can be more concise by rephrasing your words. Concise writing is easier for the reader to understand.

21. Simplify this sentence by separating it into two separate sentences.

22. Remove this word. It is not grammatically correct.

23. These words are not required and can be removed to make your essay more concise.

Our expert's overall feedback in the end:

It was a pleasure reading your essay! Thank you for submitting it to us for review.

You've done a wonderful job introducing your essay. It's very personable and engaging. I was encouraged to want to read more. A captivating introduction is one of the most important components of your essay to position you as an interesting and unique candidate.

The body of your essay effectively describes why you are interested in the school, as well as what you can offer back to the school community. However, be mindful of spelling, grammar, and punctuation errors as they suggest that you didn't take the time to review your essay before submitting it. Be sure to make use of your word processor's built-in editor to help you locate and correct these errors. Also, as you complete your final review of your essay, look for opportunities to make your wording more concise.

Your essay revisions may change your word count. Ensure that your word count adheres to the limits defined for this essay prompt.

Please work on the areas outlined above and submit another draft for review when you're ready!

Cheers,
BeMo

The following document is a final draft that was the result of multiple revisions with our admissions expert. Typically, there are two to three revisions.

6e. Final draft

Carl Sagan once said, "Somewhere, something incredible is waiting to be known." For me, this quote captures the essence of science: wondering what we are made of and what can be done with such information. I have been passionate about science since I was young and asked my parents for a microscope for Christmas. I was so interested in everything around me that I used it to look at my brother's blood, pieces of plants, and insects. I cannot remember a day during which I was not wondering how things happen, such as how we walk and how we talk. With genetics courses at school, more questions arose. Because of my fascination for the world of molecular genetics, I decided to study biotechnology, with an orientation in molecular genetics, at [removed identifier] in [removed identifier]. I am ever grateful that my parents enabled me to pursue my entire high school in English and become fully fluent, as it has tremendously helped me pursue my scientific aspirations.

I would love to study at [removed identifier], a university that has outstanding resources for scientific research and is in [removed identifier], with all its cultural diversity. I have visited [removed identifier] twice over the years, and [removed identifier] caught my attention, particularly because of its vibrant culture, its diverse population, and its openness to different cultures. Not surprisingly, [removed identifier] is known as the best city for students worldwide. Thus, [removed identifier] seems to be an ideal choice for my further education.

As a final note, over the years I have complemented my studies with social outreach. For instance, I volunteered in non-governmental organizations [(removed identifiers)] and have become an expert in the communication of sign language. I have learned so much from helping others and from being in contact with diverse people. This has encouraged me to participate in social activities related to science, such as tutoring elementary students in science. These activities helped me grow as a person. I wish to contribute these values, combined with my passion for science, to my future scientific endeavors.

Thank you very much for your interest and consideration. I tremendously look forward to the opportunity to carry out my studies in the [removed identifier] program at [removed identifier], which I would honor to the highest degree.

6f. Discussion

The applicant's first draft was a good start. Their introduction was appealing, and their essay responded fully to the prompt.

In subsequent drafts, the applicant improved several minor punctuation, grammatical, and spelling errors that detracted from the quality of their essay. Additionally, the applicant reworded several statements in their essay to make it more concise and readable. The result is a polished and professional essay ready for submission.

The supplemental essay prompt: If you had the resources and skills to address a current societal problem or challenge, what would you choose and why? (650-word limit)

7a. First draft

I have always believed in the power of education as a solution to overcoming the world's challenges. Today, our society faces issues of poverty, hunger, war, disease, and instability. The one thing that all these issues have in common is that they can be addressed through knowledge. Collectively, we can increase awareness, support governments that prioritize these issues, and lobby for changes when governments don't respond.

My respect for education developed as a child growing up with a single parent. I watched my father struggle to make ends meet. He worked hard to ensure that I would have opportunities that he didn't have to improve my own life. By prioritizing education, I would be able to support myself and any family I choose to have, and I would also contribute positively to my community. Lifting myself out of the financial distress of my childhood would also lift others. These ideals were important to my father.

Indeed, I worked hard in school, earning high grades, participating in extracurricular activities, and earning scholarships. As I continue my education, knowledge is the resource I carry with me to the future to impact societal change, and my educational experiences are the skills I have to apply that knowledge.

Part of the knowledge we achieve in our lives comes through our role models. Besides my father, the most important role model in my life has been my high school counselor, Mr. [removed identifier], who helped me navigate my first year of high school when I felt I could not meet the goals I set for myself. Mr. [removed identifier] helped me plan for post-secondary education, but in doing so he taught me through his example the type of person I wanted to become.

Originally a teacher, Mr. [removed identifier] decided to return to this calling when I was in Grade 12. He left our school and his counselor position to take a teaching role in the neighborhood where he grew up. This neighborhood, which was known for crime and poverty, represented to Mr. [removed identifier] a way to contribute solutions at the local level through education.

Through my father's and Mr. [removed identifier]'s example, I also wish to promote education, but on a global rather than local level. As a journalist, I will have an opportunity to contribute to information sharing on world scale by covering social issues and efforts to solve them. I will give a voice to the vulnerable and call out those who are actively working against solutions. Further, as a journalist I will have a deep understanding of government operations and how to leverage them toward a cause.

I don't believe that change comes about through one person. It must be achieved collectively, through education, as we teach one another, share our successes, and learn from our failures. The issues of our world will not be solved overnight. Rather, they will be solved by many actions and the efforts of countless individuals, including people like my father and Mr. [removed identifier]. We all have unique backgrounds and skills to contribute to broadening the reach of education, whether that be in our social circles, our communities, our nations, or the world. My job as a journalist will be to collect these disparate threads of information to ensure that the great ideas of the world's problem-solvers and innovators are shared.

7b. Exercise: Can you spot the errors?

Use the space below to write down the errors you have spotted. Make sure you do this before moving on to the next section. Besides identifying grammatical errors, also make note of red flags, issues with structure and flow, and so forth. Take your time and refer to *Chapter III: 7 Common Essay Errors* if necessary.

7c. List of errors

Now let's examine the errors our admissions expert identified. To help you better understand our approach, these errors will be bolded and underlined in the revised draft in the following section.

- *Weak introduction:* The opening of the essay is not inspiring. To make it memorable, the applicant should apply a creative strategy to garner the reader's attention. This strategy might be starting with a question, a quote, or a description of a transformative experience.

- *Informal wording:* Avoid cliché, colloquial, or otherwise informal wording in an essay. It is unprofessional and may not be clear to some readers.

- *Poor word choice and phrasing:* Some statements are awkward or use inaccurate words. The applicant's essay would benefit from a final review before submission to identify these issues.

- *Weak transitions:* There are poor transitions between some ideas in the essay. These instances break the flow of reading.

- *Structural improvements:* Common ideas should be organized into one paragraph. Logical paragraphs allow the reader to easily identify the essay's main ideas.

Note: **The passages in which the expert left comments or suggestions for the student to review are underlined and marked using superscript numerals. Use these numerals to reference our expert's comments/suggestions listed below the revised draft.**

7d. First revision by a BeMo admissions expert

I have always believed in the power of education as a solution to overcoming the world's challenges.[1] Today, our society faces issues of poverty, hunger, war, disease, and instability. The one thing that all these issues have in common is that they can be addressed through knowledge. Collectively, we can increase awareness, support governments that prioritize these issues, and lobby for changes when governments ~~don't~~ **do not** respond.

My respect for education developed as a child growing up with a single parent. I watched my father struggle to make **ends meet**.[2] He worked hard to ensure that I would have opportunities that he ~~didn't have to improve my own life~~[3] **did not**. By prioritizing education, I would be able to support myself and any family I choose to have, and I would also contribute positively to my community. Lifting myself out of the financial distress of my childhood would also lift others. These ideals were important to my father.

Indeed, I worked hard in school, earning high grades, participating in extracurricular activities, and earning scholarships.[4] As I continue my education,[5] knowledge is the resource I carry with me to the future to impact societal change, and my educational experiences ~~are the skills I have~~ **gave me the skills**[6] to apply that knowledge.

Part of the knowledge we achieve in our lives comes through our role models. Besides my father, the most important role model in my life has been my high school counselor, Mr. [removed identifier], who helped me navigate my first year of high school when I felt I could not meet the goals I set for myself. Mr. [removed identifier] helped me plan for post-secondary education, ~~but~~ **and**[7] in doing so he taught me through his example the type of person I wanted to become.

Originally a teacher, Mr. [removed identifier] ~~decided to return~~ **returned**[8] to this calling when I was in Grade 12. He left our school and his counselor position to take a teaching role in the neighborhood where he grew up. This neighborhood, which was

known for crime and poverty, represented to Mr. [removed identifier] a way to contribute solutions at the local level through education.[9]

Through my father's and Mr. [removed identifier]'s example, I also wish to promote education, but on a global rather than local level. As a journalist, I will have an opportunity to contribute to information sharing on world scale by ~~covering~~ **reporting on**[10] social issues and efforts to solve them. I will give a voice to the vulnerable and call out those who are actively working against solutions. Further, as a journalist I will have a deep understanding of government operations and how to leverage them toward a cause.

I ~~don't~~ **do not** believe that change comes about through one person. It must be achieved collectively, through education, as we teach one another, share our successes, and learn from our failures. The issues of our world will not be solved overnight. Rather, they will be solved by many actions and the efforts of countless individuals, including people like my father and Mr. [removed identifier]. We all have unique backgrounds and skills to contribute to broadening the reach of education, whether that be in our social circles, our communities, our nations, or the world. My job as a journalist will be to collect these disparate threads of information to ensure that the great ideas of the world's problem-solvers and innovators are shared.

Word count prior to revision: 555

Word count after revision: 552

Word count limit (school specific): 650

Expert's comments/suggestions:

1. Your introduction is the reader's first encounter with you. Make it memorable and creative. For example, start with a question, a quote, or a description of a transformative experience.

2. Avoid cliché, colloquial, or otherwise informal phrasing. It's not appropriate for a formal essay, and it might confuse some readers.

3. This phrase is awkward and doesn't lend to the quality of your essay. I recommend removing it.

4. This sentence continues the idea of the previous paragraph. To improve your essay's flow, consider combining these two paragraphs.

5. This transition from the previous sentence is abrupt. Elaborate on this sentence to lead the reader more gently from the previous sentence.

6. Be sure to use the correct wording to support your ideas. Here, you describe educational experiences as skills, which they are not. Instead, these experiences were a means to develop skills.

7. The correct word to use is "and" rather than "but." Using the correct words will make your essay's meaning more powerful rather than detracting from it with the wrong word.

8. Find opportunities to be concise. It will make your essay more polished, as well as maximize your available word count.

9. Use precise wording so that your meaning is clear to the reader.

10. This paragraph can be combined with the previous paragraph, which will also improve your essay's overall flow. Common ideas should be organized within the same paragraph.

Our expert's overall feedback in the end:

Thank you! It was a pleasure reading your essay.

My first suggestion relates to your introduction. By including a unique or creative opening statement, you can leverage the primacy effect. This concept describes the observation that people tend to recall what they first encounter. If you have a strong introductory sentence, your entire essay will be more memorable to the reader. Some strategies to consider for your introductory sentence are starting with a question, a quote, or a description of a transformative experience.

Within your essay, pay careful attention to your word choice. Avoid cliché, colloquial, or otherwise informal wording, and replace awkward or inaccurate phrasing. Your final draft should be clear and concise.

With respect to the organization of your essay, ensure that common ideas are contained within the same paragraph and that you have built effective transitions between sentences and paragraphs. Proper organization is essential to the effective flow of your essay.

Your essay revisions may change your word count. Ensure that your word count adheres to the limits defined for this essay prompt.

Please work on the areas outlined above and submit another draft for review when you're ready!

Cheers,
BeMo

The following document is a final draft that was the result of multiple revisions with our admissions expert. Typically, there are two to three revisions.

7e. Final draft

What is the solution to overcoming the world's challenges? The only answer is education. Today, our society faces issues of poverty, hunger, war, disease, and instability. The one thing that all these issues have in common is that they can be addressed through education. Collectively, we can harness education to increase awareness and approach solutions.

My respect for education developed as the child of a single parent. I watched my father struggle financially. He worked hard to ensure that I would have opportunities that he did not. By prioritizing education, I would be able to support myself and my future family, and I would also contribute positively to my community. Lifting myself out of the financial distress of my childhood would also lift others. These ideals were important to my father. Indeed, I worked hard in school, earning high grades, participating in extracurricular activities, and earning scholarships. Now, as I continue my education, knowledge is the resource I carry with me to the future to impact societal change, and my educational experiences have given me the skills to apply that knowledge.

Part of the knowledge we achieve in our lives comes through our role models. Besides my father, the most important role model in my life has been my high school counselor, Mr. [removed identifier], who helped me navigate my first year of high school when I felt I could not meet the goals I set for myself. Through his example, Mr. [removed identifier] taught me the type of person I wanted to become. Originally a teacher, Mr. [removed identifier] returned to this calling when I was in Grade 12. He left our school and his counselor position to take a teaching role in the neighborhood where he grew up. This neighborhood, which was known for crime and poverty, represented to Mr. [removed identifier] a way to contribute solutions at a local level through education.

Following my father's and Mr. [removed identifier]'s example, I also wish to promote education, but on a global rather than a personal or local level. As a journalist, I will have an opportunity to contribute to knowledge sharing on world scale by reporting on prevalent social issues and efforts to solve them. I will give a voice to the vulnerable and call out those who are actively working against solutions. Further, as a journalist I will have a deep understanding of government operations and how to leverage them toward a cause.

I do not believe that change comes about through one person. It must be achieved collectively, through education, as we teach one another, share our successes, and learn from our failures. The issues of our world will not be solved overnight. Rather, they will be solved by many actions and the efforts of countless individuals, including people like my father and Mr. [removed identifier]. We all have unique backgrounds and skills to contribute to broadening the reach of education, whether that be in our social circles, our communities, our nations, or the world. My job as a journalist will be to collect these disparate threads of information to ensure that the great ideas of the world's problem-solvers and innovators are shared.

7f. Discussion

The applicant incorporated a recommendation to make their introductory sentence more unique and creative by starting with a question. The essay's beginning is now stronger and will be more compelling to the reader.

Throughout the essay, cliché, colloquial, and other informal wording was removed to align with an essay format. Additionally, the applicant removed awkward and inaccurate phrasing to make their essay clear and concise.

Overall, the applicant's efforts to reorganize the essay into more logical paragraphs have improved transitions and benefited the flow of the essay.

The supplemental essay prompt: What factors influenced your decision to apply to [school]? Why do you think [school] is the right school for you? (650-word limit)

8a. First draft

In 2011 I started an internship at [removed identifier] in [removed identifier]. During my first week, I already was eager to dive into CT scans and iris examinations. To my chagrin, I was handed countless patient documents to file. But as I skidded across the white marble floor, running from one side of the office to console a patient and then to the other to call the insurance company, I realized these were tasks I was tremendously proud to be responsible for.

My involvement at [removed identifier] led to my desire to pursue a career in medicine. Since then, from conducting biomedical research at [removed identifier] to designing and building toys at a school for disabled children, I found myself enjoying not only the ambiance of a biology-focused setting, but also experiences where I could collaborate on projects with others. At [removed identifier], the program boasts a myriad of resources that allow me to do just that.

[Program] offers more than 380 biology courses, and through classes like Stem Cell Biology or Molecular and Genetic Approaches to Neuroscience, I would be able to explore my passion in human cell development or optogenetics, especially in clinical applications. The presence of student involvement in classes is also meaningful to me, evident through discussions and hands-on learning experiences offered by laboratory work and smaller group seminars.

I was ecstatic to see the variety of team-oriented research conducted at [program]. Like the hundeds of students at [removed identifier] who enroll in undergraduate research, I hope to contribute my curiosity and knowledge to a research team and develop an independent project. I would like to apply to the research honors program, and conduct my original research under the guide of a faculty member, just as I had done at summer research project at [removed identifier].

Additionally, what made [removed identifier] distinctive from [removed identifier] were the distribution requirements while studying biological sciences. A good portion of the [removed identifier] curriculum includes a focus on physical and life sciences, which were concentrations I had a particular interest for at [removed identifier]. In the STEM field classes offered at my high school, I loved being able to connect classroom theories and apply them to tangible, real-world issues. At [removed identifier], the intimate 20-people classroom setting with enthusiastic students and faculty will contribute to the kind of dynamic learning environment that caters to me as a student.

Perhaps what makes [removed identifier] one of my top choices is its pre-professional med program and business minor. At a college fair at my high school, a [removed identifier] representative discussed the unique opportunity to minor in business while majoring in another academic subject; this would not only supplement the major, but also build a foundation in entrepreneurship for the life sciences as well. This opportunity would allow me, as an aspiring pre-med student, to gain invaluable experience in business and entrepreneurship. This minor would provide me with invaluable skills in any administrative workplace after college.

As a hopeful [removed identifier] student, I'm eager to accept the abounding opportunities that will allow me to further my knowledge in biological sciences.

8b. Exercise: Can you spot the errors?

Use the space below to write down the errors you have spotted. Make sure you do this before moving on to the next section. Besides identifying grammatical errors, also make note of red flags, issues with structure and flow, and so forth. Take your time and refer to *Chapter III: 7 Common Essay Errors* if necessary.

8c. List of errors

Now let's examine the errors our admissions expert identified. To help you better understand our approach, these errors will be bolded and underlined in the revised draft in the following section.

- *Minor errors in word choice and phrasing:* The language and structure of the essay needs to be appropriate for the format. Replacing informal language and reorganizing some sentences for clarity will improve the reader's experience. Also, during a final review, ensure that the correct words are used and that no words are missing.

- *Wrong tense:* Some minor tense issues at the end of the essay can be avoided with rewording. The applicant uses the past tense when the present tense is more powerful and appropriate.

- *Not concise:* The applicant can make their writing more concise by removing unnecessary and redundant words.

- *Punctuation errors:* The essay contains minor punctuation errors that will be distracting to the reader. It is a good practice to review the entire essay before finalizing it to correct any punctuation errors. Do not forget to check for duplicate spaces between words and sentences.

- *Minor grammatical errors:* Minor errors in grammar can impact the ease of reading. Fixing these errors will make for a more polished essay. Always set aside time to complete a final end-to-end review of your essay before submitting it.

- *Ineffective transitions:* Transitions between sentences and paragraphs can be improved. The essay should demonstrate a natural and logical progression from one idea to the next.

- *Weak conclusion:* The conclusion needs to be strong as it represents the admission committee's last impression of the applicant. The applicant should expand their conclusion and end with a memorable statement.

<u>Note</u>: **The passages in which the expert left comments or suggestions for the student to review are underlined and marked using superscript numerals. Use these numerals to reference our expert's comments/suggestions listed below the revised draft.**

8d. First revision by a BeMo admissions expert

In 2011,[1] I started an internship at [removed identifier] in [removed identifier]. During my first week, I ~~already~~[2] was eager to dive into CT scans and iris examinations. To my chagrin, I was handed countless patient documents to file. **However,**[3] as I skidded across the white marble floor, running from one side of the office to console a patient and then to the other to call the insurance company, I realized **I was tremendously proud to be responsible for these tasks** ~~these were tasks that I was tremendously proud to be responsible~~.[4]

My involvement at [removed identifier] led to my desire to pursue a career in medicine. **Since then, from conducting biomedical research at [removed identifier] to designing and building toys at a school for disabled children, I found myself enjoying not only the ambiance of a biology-focused setting, but also experiences where I could collaborate on projects with others.**[5] **At [removed identifier], the program boasts a myriad of resources that allow me to do just that.**[6]

[Program] offers more than 380 biology courses, and through classes like Stem Cell Biology **or Molecular**[7] and Genetic Approaches to Neuroscience, I **can** ~~would be able to~~[8] explore my passion **for** ~~in~~[9] human cell development or optogenetics, especially in clinical applications. The presence of student involvement in classes is also meaningful to me, evident through discussions and hands-on learning experiences offered by laboratory work and smaller group seminars.

I was ecstatic to see the variety of team-oriented research conducted at **[program]. Like**[10] the **hundreds**[11] of students at [removed identifier] who enroll in undergraduate research, I hope to contribute my curiosity and knowledge to a research team and develop an independent project. I would like to apply to the research honors **program**[12] and conduct my original research under the guide of a faculty member, just as I had done **in my** ~~at~~[13] summer research project at [removed identifier].

Additionally, what made [removed identifier] distinctive from [removed identifier] were the distribution requirements while studying biological sciences.[14] A good portion of the [removed identifier] curriculum includes a focus on physical and life sciences, which were concentrations ~~I had a~~ **of particular interest to me** ~~for~~[15] in high school. In the STEM field classes offered at my high school, I loved being able to connect classroom theories and apply them to tangible, real-world issues. At [removed identifier], the intimate 20-**person** ~~people~~[16] classroom setting with enthusiastic students and faculty will contribute to the kind of dynamic learning environment that caters to me as a student.

~~Perhaps what makes [removed identifier] one of my top choices is its~~ **[Removed identifier]'s pre-professional med program and business minor make it one of my top choices**.[17] At a college fair at my high school, a [removed identifier] representative discussed the unique opportunity to minor in business while majoring in another academic subject; this **option**[18] ~~would~~ **not only supplements**[19] the major, but also **builds**[20] a foundation in entrepreneurship for the life sciences as well. This opportunity **will** ~~would~~[21] allow me, as an aspiring pre-med student, to gain invaluable experience in business and entrepreneurship. **Further, it will** ~~This minor would~~[22] provide me with invaluable skills **I can use**[23] in any administrative workplace after college.

As a hopeful [removed identifier] student, I'm eager to accept the abounding opportunities that will allow me to further my knowledge in biological sciences.[24]

Word count prior to revision: 512

Word count after revision: 508

Word count limit (school specific): 650

Expert's comments/suggestions:

1. The comma is missing here. Commas help to organize sentences and make them easier to read.

2. Remove unnecessary words to make your writing more concise. This word is awkward in the sentence. Removing it will not impact your intended meaning.

3. Avoid starting sentences with "But" as this is a formal essay. Replace this word with "However" or a similar transition word.

4. Changing your word order makes the sentence easier to read and more concise.

5. You've done a wonderful job here of including examples leading to your interest in medicine as a career.

6. This is an excellent transition statement. It sums up the current paragraph and logically leads the reader to the next paragraph.

7. There was an extra space between these two words. Sometimes it's difficult to locate extra spaces depending on the font you're using. However, your word processing application likely has an editing tool that will flag these instances for you. You can also run a search for duplicate spaces using your Find tool.

8. Look for opportunities to make your essay more concise. Here, you can replace four words with one word. This change will also increase your available word count.

9. Be sure to use the correct words. Common mistakes in first drafts, such as using the wrong word, can be easily identified by doing a careful review of your entire essay after other updates are complete.

10. Watch for extra spaces between words. Your final essay needs to be polished and professional before submitting it to the admissions committee.

11. This word contains a spelling error. It's valuable to use your word processor's spell-checking tool after completing your document to locate any final errors. However, you still need to do a final end-to-end review of your essay before submitting it.

12. The comma after "program" is not required since you aren't joining two independent clauses here.

13. This phrase was incomplete. I have included my suggested wording change.

14. This paragraph begins abruptly after the previous paragraph. A thoughtful transition sentence will assist the reader in moving from the previous paragraph to this one.

15. Rephrasing your words here will add polish to your essay and make it easier for the reader to understand your meaning.

16. "Person," not "people," is the correct word to use.

17. Avoid using the word "perhaps" as it suggests indecisiveness. Rewriting this sentence also makes it more concise.

18. Ensure that your meaning is clear for the reader. Sometimes using the word "this" can introduce confusion if it's not further defined.

19. Use the present tense instead of the past tense. It's more powerful and appropriate to the content.

20. This word needs to be updated to reflect other recommended changes.

21. Change the tense for a more powerful sentence.

22. This sentence requires a more obvious transition from the previous sentence. Also, the past tense is used here again and should be changed to the present tense.

23. A few additional words will provide clarity for the reader.

24. Your concluding paragraph is your last opportunity to impress the admissions committee. Strengthen this section by making it longer and ending on a memorable note. Be sure to summarize the key points of your essay in the conclusion.

Our expert's overall feedback in the end:

Excellent job on your first draft! You've clearly outlined your reasons for applying to this school and the experiences you hope to gain as a student. I appreciated reading about your interests, including enrolling in specific courses and applying to the research honors program. You also demonstrated that you're familiar with the school's culture by highlighting how you will participate in the classroom and interact with fellow students in the program.

Your introduction is strong. By starting with an example of a personal experience related to your desired program of study, you immediately engage the reader. Your conclusion is not as strong and would benefit from some additional work. Expand the conclusion beyond one sentence and aim to make it memorable for the reader. The conclusion is also where you can remind the reader of your key points.

Before you submit your final draft to the admissions committee, be sure to review your essay in detail and use the spell-check and editing tools available in your word processing program. Your essay has several minor punctuation and grammatical errors, as well as spelling errors, which could distract the reader from your message.

Your essay revisions may change your word count. Ensure that your word count adheres to the limits defined for this essay prompt.

Please work on the areas outlined above and submit another draft for review when you're ready!

Cheers,
BeMo

The following document is a final draft that was the result of multiple revisions with our admissions expert. Typically, there are two to three revisions.

8e. Final draft

In 2011, I started an internship at [removed identifier] in [removed identifier]. During my first week, I was eager to dive into CT scans and iris examinations. To my chagrin, I was handed countless patient documents to file. However, as I skidded across the white marble floor, running from one side of the office to console a patient and then to the other to call the insurance company, I realized I was tremendously proud to be responsible for these tasks.

My involvement at [removed identifier] led to my desire to pursue a career in medicine. Since then, from conducting biomedical research at [removed identifier] to designing and building toys at a school for disabled children, I found myself enjoying not only the ambiance of a biology-focused setting, but also experiences where I could collaborate on projects with others. At [removed identifier], the program boasts a myriad of resources that allow me to do just that.

[Removed identifier] offers more than 380 biology courses, and through classes like Stem Cell Biology or Molecular and Genetic Approaches to Neuroscience, I can explore my passion for human cell development or optogenetics, especially in clinical applications. The presence of student involvement in classes is also meaningful to me, evident through discussions and hands-on learning experiences offered by laboratory work and smaller group seminars.

I was ecstatic to see the variety of team-oriented research conducted at [removed identifier]. Like the hundreds of students at [removed identifier] who enroll in undergraduate research, I hope to contribute my curiosity and knowledge to a research team and develop an independent project. I would like to apply to the research honors program and conduct my original research under the guidance of a faculty member, just as I had done in my summer research project at [removed identifier]. The availability of this option is appealing to me as an avid learner.

Distribution requirements for studying biological sciences at [removed identifier] include a focus on physical and life sciences, which were concentrations of particular interest to me in high school. In the STEM field classes offered at my high school, I loved being able to connect classroom theories and apply them to tangible, real-world issues. At [removed identifier], the intimate 20-person classroom setting with enthusiastic students and faculty will contribute to the kind of dynamic learning environment that caters to me as a student.

[Removed identifier]'s pre-professional med program and practical business minor make it one of my top choices. At a college fair at my high school, a [removed identifier] representative discussed the unique opportunity to minor in business while majoring in another academic subject; this option not only supplements the major, but also builds a foundation in entrepreneurship for the life sciences as well. This opportunity will allow me, as an aspiring pre-med student, to gain invaluable experience in business and entrepreneurship. Further, it will provide me with invaluable skills I can use in any administrative workplace after college.

As a hopeful [removed identifier] student, I am eager to accept the abounding opportunities that will allow me to further my knowledge in biological sciences. I especially look forward to participating in the honors research program, studying a curriculum focused on physical and life sciences, interacting with my fellow students in small classes, and earning a business minor to supplement my degree. I am confident that [removed identifier]'s unmatched program and culture will develop me into a knowledgeable, skilled, and versatile professional.

8f. Discussion

The first draft of this essay was strong. To introduce the essay, the applicant recounted an experience in a clinical setting that prompted an interest in the biological sciences. By sharing this transformative experience, the applicant engaged the reader from the start. The essay introduction is critical to get right because this is the admission committee's first impression of the applicant.

In the body of the essay, the applicant effectively presented reasons for applying to this specific school. They noted an interest in the honors research program, a curriculum focused on physical and life sciences, small classes promoting student interaction, and the availability of a business minor to supplement the degree. Minor errors in spelling, punctuation, and grammar were corrected for the final draft, making the essay polished and professional.

Finally, the applicant expanded on their original conclusion to recount key points from their essay that they wanted to emphasize to the admissions committee. The final draft effectively sums up the applicant's essay and leaves a positive impression with the reader.

CHAPTER VI

How to Brainstorm for Your Personal Statement and Supplemental Essays

Congratulations on successfully journeying with us through the revision process for a number of real essays. Now, it is time to create your own, and we hope you are as excited as we are!

Chapter VI: How to Brainstorm for Your Personal Statement and Supplemental Essays, Chapter VII: Key Components for Your Outline, and *Chapter VIII: How to Write Your Own from Scratch* are modeled after our brainstorming consultation sessions. The purpose behind such sessions is to give students the opportunity to collaborate with a BeMo admissions expert in gathering and organizing the pieces of their story, which will eventually form the contents of their personal statement. Since the consultation session is conducted in two parts, brainstorming the story content and creating an outline, these three chapters will follow this structure. *Chapter VI: How to Brainstorm for Your Personal Statement and Supplemental Essays* will show you how to reflect on your life experiences and identify those that are significant and relevant. You will then learn about the structure of an essay in *Chapter VII: Key Components for Your Outline* and use the product from this brainstorming exercise to create your essay outline in *Chapter VIII: How to Write Your Own from Scratch*.

Are you ready? Here we go!

To start the brainstorming process, we recommend that you reflect on your life experiences in chronological order, beginning with significant childhood events, moving gradually toward the present, and eventually thinking about the future. The purpose of this exercise is to help you recall and isolate significant moments of realization, learning, transformation, and decision-making that shaped you as a person and will continue to inform your future goals.

Use the following prompts to guide you as you reflect on the events and experiences in your life that have led you here.

a) What was your childhood like? Were there any significant experiences?

Although you may not include any childhood experiences in your outline or final essay, it is a good place to start when brainstorming. Once you reflect on these experiences, it will become clearer to you whether they are relevant to your journey, and whether you want to share them with the admissions committee. If you do decide to include them, it will then be your job to connect the dots between these early experiences and later ones to weave together a coherent story. Let's look at a few potential examples you may use:

- *Location:* Where you grew up may be instrumental in shaping your current passions and goals. Did you grow up in a rural neighborhood where access to services was a problem? Or, did you live in an urban environment where you experienced great diversity but also saw social and economic disparities?

- *Family:* A topic that many students shy away from is discussing their family, but this is an important part of who you are. Whether you grew up tending to a family member who was ill or you endured family struggles that were critical in shaping your values, your family might be one of the biggest reasons why you are pursuing a particular field of study. If this is the case, these experiences may become relevant when you are responding to the essay prompts for your personal statement or supplemental essays.

- *Immigration:* Immigration or your family's journey to a new home is a common experience many of us have. For some, the struggles they endured and the experience of beginning anew could have been meaningful and motivating.

- *Personal experiences:* Typically, any experience that exposed you to your desired field of study has potential. Perhaps you recall an interaction that was impactful to you or inspired you to get involved in the field in some way. If this is something you can relate to, think about what you gained from these experiences and how they propelled you forward.

b) What were your high school experiences?

For many, high school is the time when you start to develop as an independent individual and your decision about your future career is set. Besides establishing your academic interests, you likely also engaged in extracurricular activities that exposed you to your field of interest. The brainstorming here is thus beneficial for preparing your application as a whole. Let's look at a few examples you may use:

- *Academics:* Think about which subjects in school you liked best and did well in. Perhaps you also recall having a conversation with one or more high school teachers or a counselor who guided you to take certain courses, encouraged you to volunteer, or inspired you to choose a particular career.

- *Volunteering:* A volunteer experience is often your first exposure to 'real life' professional settings or issues. For example, a student who volunteered for Habitat for Humanity might become aware of societal issues regarding housing and the barriers to housing faced by many low-income families. Someone who volunteers at a clinic may notice the demand for more healthcare providers. Though your role may not be significant, your takeaways are! Therefore, always reflect on what you learned and how that motivates you to serve other people.

- *Sports and other extracurricular activities:* Becoming involved in sports and other extracurricular activities is celebrated in applications. Why? Because they usually expose you to collaborative environments where you learn how to work with others. Even if such experiences may not fit into your personal statement or supplemental essays, they can certainly be included in your activities section in Common App.

c) What were your university or college experiences?

If you have previously attended university or college, this time represents recent and impactful experiences. Let's look at a few examples you could use:

- *Volunteering:* In college, the volunteering roles you took on were likely more involved and offered greater insight into your future career direction. After identifying these experiences, also reflect on what you learned from each. Choose activities that demonstrate a wide range of skills and qualities.

- *Shadowing:* Candidates who have a lot of shadowing experiences tend to want to list them all, but you should reflect on the ones you have and highlight one or two that were the most impactful. Remember, quality over quantity.

- *Research:* Research experience is also appreciated since the advancement of knowledge depends on it. If you have done research, it would be in your best interest to include it in your application. What was your research about, and why was it important? What were your roles and responsibilities? Were there any challenges, and how did you overcome them? What were your research results? Last but not least, what did you learn from this experience?

- *Extracurricular activities:* As you did for your high school years, you also want to reflect on your extracurricular involvement during university. Do not list your activities like you would on a CV or resume. Only write down the ones that are noteworthy. You may not be able to discuss them in your personal statement, but you may still be able to use them in your supplemental essays or in the activities section in Common App.

- *Award(s):* Did you receive an award that you are proud of? How competitive was it? Why were you given this award, and what does it reveal about you? How is it tied to other experiences you may have already brainstormed about? Again, write this all down so you can see if and how it fits into your overall story.

d) Do you have any areas of discrepancies?

An important question that you must ask yourself is whether there are any discrepancies within your application that may be flagged by admissions. If they do exist, you want to clarify them strategically in your essay. You must address any discrepancy directly without tiptoeing around it, and importantly, make sure you discuss how you overcame it and what you learned from it. Let's look at some examples of such discrepancies:

- *Academic break or gap:* Having an academic break or gap is more common than most people think. If you took a break during or between degrees, acknowledge it and proactively address why you needed the time off, what you did during that time, and what you learned.

- *Poor grades:* Another common discrepancy that you might want to address is a poor grade in one or a few courses, provided that this is not reflective of your entire transcript. Again, you want to ensure that you address the reason behind the poor academic performance, what you did to overcome this, and what you learned. Show how you turned this into a learning opportunity.

e) What are your future plans?

Another question to consider when you brainstorm is whether you have any immediate plans or goals that you feel admissions should know about. Perhaps you have been invited to give a talk or present your work at a conference, or you will have an upcoming publication. Maybe you were just hired for a job related to your desired field of study, but you haven't started working yet. If there is something that has yet to happen but demonstrates a characteristic you are proud of, feel free to share it.

Unless otherwise detailed, the experiences you brainstormed should all connect to the main question of any application essay: Why have you decided to pursue this field of study? Additionally, your experiences should demonstrate why you are suited for the profession. If you are asked more specific questions, be sure to use only the most relevant experiences to answer them. A heartwarming story with valuable insights is meaningless if it does not ultimately address the question at hand.

Happy brainstorming!

CHAPTER VII

Key Components for Your Outline

N ow that you have brainstormed ideas for your personal statement and other components of your application that require you to share your experiences, you are one step closer to creating your outline. Before you start this next step, it is imperative for you to understand how a personal statement should be structured and how the contents should be organized. We have discussed this briefly in earlier chapters, but let's take a closer look at what each section should encompass.

1. Introduction

The first sentence and paragraph are critical! This is the first introduction you give the reviewers about yourself and your motivations for pursuing a particular profession. How you start your personal statement can make or break your essay.

Making a strong first impression is important at every stage of the application process. The primacy effect dictates that the first impression you make on someone, through writing or in person, will cement their judgments about you as a person, whether positive or negative. This means that even if the rest of your essay is strong, it may not be enough to overturn the impression left by a weak opening paragraph or statement. Thus, your introductory sentence and paragraph must be compelling, thoughtful, and attention-grabbing to ensure you are making a positive impression on the reader right from the start and make them want to continue reading your essay.

Below, we provide examples of a weak opening statement and a strong opening statement for you to see the difference for yourself.

Weak: "I have wanted to become an engineer since I was 5 years old."

This sentence is clear and direct, but it is so commonly used that it will neither stand out, nor capture the reader's attention. By pinpointing the career decision in the distant past, it also limits the applicant's ability to engage in further discussion about their journey toward their chosen profession.

Strong: "I stood in front of the audience, anxious to begin my ballet performance."

This sentence is setting the scene for an anecdote that can effectively pique the reader's curiosity, making them want to find out more about the applicant's story. Even though it does not mention the applicant's desired field of study, its uniqueness sets the writer apart from the crowd. Once you have the reader's attention, you can then draw a connection between this anecdote and your desired field of study. Some effective examples of this strategy can be found in *Chapter IV: 10 Personal Statement Examples: From First Draft to Acceptance-Magnet Final Draft.*

Though sequentially the introductory paragraph comes first, we recommend that you write this paragraph after the body paragraphs. This is because once your body paragraphs are written, you will know exactly which themes you must introduce and have a clearer idea of effective ways to do this. Working backwards, you will then find it easier to craft an eye-catching opening sentence to grab the reader's attention.

2. Body paragraphs

The outline of your body paragraphs should come first. Typically, you will have anywhere from two to four body paragraphs in your essay. Each of these can focus on a particular experience. In your exploration of each experience, you should explain how your interactions changed your approach to a problem, informed your views, taught you a new skill, or demonstrated something that pushed you further along on your road to pursuing a profession.

Focus on fewer, rather than more, experiences. Do not be tempted to use your personal statement as a chance to restate your entire CV or resume as doing so will limit your ability to fully explore each experience. If you cannot expand on why each experience was important, the reviewer will gain no new insights about your life, personality, skills, or motivation. Therefore, choose no more than three experiences to include in your essay. In rare instances, you can even focus on one experience for your entire essay, but this needs to be done strategically, and only if through that one experience you are able to demonstrate multiple facets of yourself. Although this proves to be more challenging, it will allow you to describe the experience in great depth and fully explore why it's significant.

Here is a sample outline of the body paragraphs:

Body paragraph 1: Dance. Details about practice and performance are listed. Connection with a dance teacher is mentioned, highlighting the importance of mentorship in education. Lessons learned, which must be shown through examples. Include perseverance and accepting new challenges.

Body paragraph 2: Interest in dance led to an opportunity with low-income youths. Details are described and showcase the lessons learned through this experience, as well as how they led to considering social policy as a career. For example, learning how income affects opportunities.

221

Body paragraph 3: Experience increased interest in social policy, leading to an internship. Highlight a specific interaction. Articulate what was learned from that interaction: an appreciation for and growing skills in communication, advocacy, and mentorship.

3. Transitional phrases

Though transitional phrases do not constitute their own paragraphs, but rather link paragraphs, we feel that they are important enough to warrant a separate discussion. You should be thinking about how you will transition from one idea to the next even as you are creating your outline.

Your personal statement should not read like a list of bullet points that are disconnected from one another. Using effective transitions will give your essay flow and ensure that your readers can follow the progression of your story. Ideally, the life events that you discuss will also have a common thread that makes the entire narrative cohesive.

Continuing to use the outline above as an example, you can see how one experience leads to the next, clearly showing the student's thought process and motivations as they move from one experience to another.

For examples of effective transitions, we refer you to the final drafts of personal statements and supplemental essays in *Chapter IV: 10 Personal Statement Examples: From First Draft to Acceptance-Magnet Final Draft* and *Chapter V: 8 Supplemental Essay Examples.* There are many examples of transitional statements you can use to connect the different paragraphs in your essay:

- "In addition to" or "Additionally"

- "Therefore"

- "Alongside"

- "I also decided to"

- "My experience in X led to curiosity about Y, so I decided to pursue Y"

- "In order to learn more about A, I pursued B"
- "Furthermore"

4. Discrepancies

If you have any significant academic discrepancies or breaks, you should address them proactively. If you integrate this information into your personal statement or supplemental essay, the paragraph right before your concluding paragraph should be used to discuss discrepancies or breaks in a concise and strategic manner. Alternatively, you may address the discrepancies or breaks in response to an essay prompt about other information you would like the admissions committee to know.

Examples of what should be discussed:

- Any failed or withdrawn courses, or significantly lower grades
- Time taken off that was not spent either studying or working
- Any instances of academic misconduct that were investigated in your past, such as plagiarism

If you are feeling uncertain about how best to discuss discrepancies, here are some tips to make the process less intimidating:

- State what the discrepancy is clearly and directly. There is no need to hedge your words. The admissions committee will appreciate your honesty.

- Explain the reason behind the discrepancy. In a few sentences or less, tell the committee what happened that led to the academic setback. Again, this needs to be done directly and concisely. Factors to consider are personal illness, financial hardship, family issues, poor focus, or overcommitment. Be careful about how you word this since you do not want to present yourself as someone who makes excuses or tries to rationalize irresponsible or unethical behavior.

- Turn the reader's attention toward what you did to rectify the situation. Show the admissions committee exactly how you recognized the error and took action to correct your course.

- Finally, and most importantly, point out what tools you have gained and what strategies you have in place to ensure that a situation like this never occurs again. If you find yourself in another difficult situation, you must be able to quickly recognize and respond to it. As a professional, you will routinely face obstacles, but your performance should not suffer.

Use these tips to help you address any discrepancies in a positive and proactive manner. Again, communicate that the discrepancy was a learning opportunity and that it ultimately strengthened your character.

5. Conclusion

After you have outlined your body paragraphs, you can begin work on the outline of your conclusion. This paragraph is as important as the introduction since it relays your final message to the reader. The recency effect dictates that people tend to recall the latest information more accurately than older information. This means that reviewers will remember what you say here in more detail than all the other parts of your essay. Therefore, make your conclusion as informative and powerful as you can.

Your concluding paragraph should not only help the reader recall the main ideas and themes of your essay, but it should also give the reader a lasting impression of you as a candidate and leave them wanting more. Take a look at the essay conclusions in *Chapter IV: 10 Personal Statement Examples: From First Draft to Acceptance-Magnet Final Draft* for examples of creative and effective ways to end a personal statement.

To craft the strongest concluding paragraph to your essay, consider including the following:

- A creative summary of the experiences that have solidified your desire to pursue a profession, including the skills and abilities you have garnered along the way

- A synthesis of the important lessons you have learned

- A callback to your opening anecdote to unify the essay

- A winning final sentence to end with something exciting and hopeful that leaves the reader wanting more

    o If you can achieve this, the reviewers will want to interview you so they can continue to ask you questions and find out more about you.

    o The concluding statement can be an amalgamation of the callback to your opening anecdote and an outlook onto your future. Example: "As an aspiring social policy specialist, I am now at the same place I was before beginning that dance performance: on the precipice of an exciting journey, and ready to tackle the challenges along the way." This statement not only circles back to the initial anecdote, but also connects it to the applicant's readiness for the challenges of school and a career in social policy.

Now that you have had a chance to brainstorm about your life experiences and have a better idea about how to structure your essay, the last chapter will help you to draft an outline and finally begin writing your personal statement!

CHAPTER VIII

How to Write Your Own from Scratch

In this chapter, you will learn how to structure your ideas into an outline before beginning to write. Though it may be tempting, do not skip this important step! The outline will make your essay-writing process focused and efficient.

Throughout this exercise, be sure to refer to the structures and key components outlined in *Chapter VI: How to Brainstorm for Your Personal Statement and Supplemental Essays* and *Chapter VII: Key Components for Your Outline*. Additionally, revisit the notes you made on all the errors you spotted and those the experts identified in *Chapter IV: 10 Personal Statement Examples: From First Draft to Acceptance-Magnet Final Draft*. Having these important concepts fresh in your mind will make this process smoother and ultimately save you time on revisions.

As you begin to work on your outline, understand that this might take more than one sitting. If you get stuck, try reflecting again on your experiences and what you learned from them. It's okay to realize that an experience you noted down was not as important or relevant as you initially thought. It can still be included in the outline and later removed as you develop and refine your draft. For the purposes of this exercise, let the question "Why do you want to pursue your field of study?" guide you. Although the application system will provide you with a list of prompts for your personal statement, these will likely include prompts about your background and interests, among other topics, as well as an open prompt. Your completion of this exercise will give you an initial start to answering these standard prompts, or you can repurpose the content for one of the other prompts in the list. Regardless of the specific prompt, always remember to tell the reader who you are as a person and what your values are.

Before we proceed, grab a pen or a pencil and get ready to write!

Are you ready? Here we go!

This exercise is laid out in the order that the sections will appear in your essay. However, we are going to ask that you work on the outline of the body paragraphs *first* and then return to this. Why? Because at this stage you are still not sure about what experiences you might discuss in your essay, so you cannot possibly know the most effective way to introduce those ideas and themes.

Introduction: When you are ready, begin to outline a captivating introduction for the two to three experiences your essay will focus on in the body paragraphs. Remember, the first sentence will make or break your essay. Think of a creative way to get the reader's attention.

_____

_____

_____

_____

_____

_____

_____

_____

_____

_____

_____

_____

_____

_____

_____

_____

_____

_____

First experience that motivated your decision: This first experience tends to be the 'aha' moment when you first discovered an interest in your field of study. Be sure to describe **(a)** the experience, **(b)** what you learned from it, and **(c)** why this experience is important for your future. In addition, jot down ways in which you might transition into the subsequent topic. Note that you are still outlining key ideas and not yet writing the first draft.

_____

_____

_____

_____

_____

_____

_____

_____

_____

_____

_____

_____

_____

_____

_____

_____

_____

_____

Second experience that motivated your decision: This tends to be an experience in which you further explored your field of study and confirmed that it is the career path you want to take. Be sure to describe **(a)** the experience, **(b)** what you learned from it, and **(c)** why this experience is important for your future. Also, jot down ways in which you might transition into the subsequent topic. Note that you are still outlining key ideas and not yet writing the first draft.

_____

_____

_____

_____

_____

_____

_____

_____

_____

_____

_____

_____

_____

_____

_____

_____

_____

_____

_____

_____

Third experience that motivated your decision: This experience is often one that reaffirms your passion toward your field of study. As you will be demonstrating multiple qualities along the way, keep in mind that you want to showcase a diverse set of characteristics and skills. Be sure to describe **(a)** the experience, **(b)** what you learned from it, and **(c)** why this experience is important for your future. Also, jot down ways in which you might transition into the subsequent topic. Note that you are still outlining key ideas and not yet writing the first draft.

_____

_____

_____

_____

_____

_____

_____

_____

_____

_____

_____

_____

_____

_____

_____

_____

_____

Areas of discrepancies: Now that you have chosen the experiences that were instrumental in shaping your decision to pursue your field of study, you can address any areas of discrepancies. Remember, these are areas that you feel might hinder your chances of acceptance and need to be addressed. Be strategic and direct when you do this. Describe **(a)** what the discrepancy was, **(b)** how you overcame or moved past it, **(c)** what you learned from the experience, and **(c)** how you will benefit from this learning in the future. Skip this section if there are no discrepancies you wish to discuss.

_____

_____

_____

_____

_____

_____

_____

_____

_____

_____

_____

_____

_____

_____

_____

_____

_____

_____

Future plans: Optionally, you can also dedicate a paragraph to discussing any upcoming opportunities that you feel will enable you to gain more insight and experience relevant to your field of study. For example, you may be starting a related volunteer or paid position, or you may have joined a professional association in the field. Be sure to discuss **(a)** the opportunity, **(b)** what your role will be, and **(c)** how this will contribute to your skill set or character.

Conclusion: Once you have an outline of the introduction and body paragraphs, you need to think of a strong conclusion. Be sure to **(a)** creatively summarize the key themes and values you learned, **(b)** revisit the opening statement for cohesion, and **(c)** end with a statement that leaves the reader wanting more.

_____

_____

_____

_____

_____

_____

_____

_____

_____

_____

_____

_____

_____

_____

_____

_____

_____

_____

_____

Now that you have taken the time to create a roadmap of your personal statement, take a break and give yourself a pat on the back – seriously! This short break will allow you to clear out any frustrations and memory blockages you may have had when recalling past experiences. Let the words settle in and give yourself some time to reflect before you proceed. Grab a healthy snack if you need to.

Once you have recharged and perhaps even thought of better ways to approach your essay, you can begin connecting the ideas in your outline and putting the first draft together. Start by stringing together the sentences within paragraphs, then use transitions to stitch together each paragraph. Recall that you will have a word limit, so be sure to be concise.

Although having a strong outline will make the process smoother, you will inevitably encounter bumps along the way as you transition from your outline to a first draft. During this process, if you happen to think of a more relevant key experience or more meaningful takeaways, feel free to revise your outline. However, always be sure to outline first before writing out the draft. It is not uncommon for students to discard drafts they've made and go back to the drawing table. Don't be afraid of large revisions because they tend to improve the quality of the overall essay as you learn from your initial mistakes. As always, if you feel stuck, go back to *Chapter VI: How to Brainstorm for Your Personal Statement and Supplemental Essays* and *Chapter VII: Key Components for Your Outline* and review the key components that will make your personal statement more effective!

Once you have completed the draft, read your essay critically from beginning to end, finding ways to make each section, if not each sentence, stronger and more concise. We suggest reading it five to 10 times prior to handing it over to an expert to proofread.

You now have your first draft. What next? We'll discuss the last ingredient to a successful personal statement in the next chapter.

CHAPTER IX

The Final Secret of Successful Applicants

Most successful applicants do something beyond what's possible with this book alone. They go that extra mile to make every aspect of their application flawless because their career depends on it. They understand that they have only one chance to make a fantastic first impression. They know that the time, money, and energy spent at this stage is an investment in their future. What do successful applicants do that's missed by those who get rejected?

They ask for a second set of eyes to look at their personal statement and supplemental essays, as well as every aspect of their application before pressing that submit button. Every great writer has an editor. You can also benefit from having an expert look at your applications and provide you with objective feedback. It's the only way to make improvements to your essays. Expert feedback will also certainly help you improve your writing skills, which you will need to excel in your future profession. So, let us tell you how our college application programs work.

Step 1 – Writer's block busting strategy session

We normally start with a strategy session where we help you brainstorm ideas for your personal statement, supplemental essays, or any other written component of your applications.

During the one-to-one video conferencing session, we ask you specific questions to find out more about you and your past experiences. We then help you to organize your experiences into a narrative that tells your unique story, and we give you a roadmap to help you start your first draft.

Step 2 – The review process

Once you have written your first draft and sent it in to us, one of our admissions experts will review your work in detail. We go over your documents word by word and provide you with written feedback on word choice, grammar, spelling, flow, and structure, and identify any red flags. We even give suggestions on how to make your documents admissions-committee-friendly. We won't hold back because we want to make sure you have a chance to fix the issues before it's too late. Once we've triple-checked the work, we return the document to you with all our suggestions within two to three business days.

Step 3 – Unlimited reviews

While some of our students might be able to write a compelling essay on their first attempt, others may require more time and revisions. Regardless, we keep working with you for as long as necessary until we are confident that your application documents are ready for submission. We will explicitly tell you when they are ready, so you never have to wonder whether or not it's time to submit.

Step 4 – Unlimited mock interviews + expert feedback

The interview stage, when required, is the most challenging hurdle. Like most applicants, you may not know what you should expect or how you will react in this stressful environment. What if you get nervous and forget what to say? What if you don't know the right answer? What if your voice cracks? What if you sweat like a marathon runner? What if, what if, what if …? BeMo first became known for its interview preparation programs because we have actual interview experts that can coach you on everything from what to say, how to say it, and when to say it, to how to make eye contact, and much more. During your interview preparation, we offer unlimited mock interviews plus expert feedback until we are confident that you are going to ace your interviews.

BeMo's Bold Guarantees:

In case you're on the fence at all, we want to note that all our programs come with guarantees. Go to BeMoUndergrad.com to learn more and enroll now or schedule a free strategy call to talk to one of our team members first.

Whether you decide to work with us or not, we hope this book helps you craft compelling application documents, so you never have to go through this process again. If you do decide to work with us, we look forward to journeying with you!

CHAPTER X

Bonus Resources

Here are additional resources to help you prepare for your applications.

Visit BeMo.Blog for our entire collection of blogs written by our senior admissions experts.

Ultimate Guide to Creating a Common App Essay
https://bemoacademicconsulting.com/blog/common-app-essay

How to Write a College Essay: Tips and Examples
https://bemoacademicconsulting.com/blog/how-to-write-a-college-essay

College Essay Examples: The Best Examples
https://bemoacademicconsulting.com/blog/sample-college-essays

Your Definitive Guide to Supplemental College Application Essays
https://bemoacademicconsulting.com/blog/supplemental-college-essays

College Essay Topics
https://bemoacademicconsulting.com/blog/college-essay-topics

How to Start a College Essay: Your Guide
https://bemoacademicconsulting.com/blog/how-to-start-a-college-essay

College Essay Introduction Examples
https://bemoacademicconsulting.com/blog/college-essay-introduction-examples

Expert College Essay Tips to Help You Stand Out
https://bemoacademicconsulting.com/blog/college-essay-tips

College Diversity Essay Examples
https://bemoacademicconsulting.com/blog/college-diversity-essay-examples

How to Ace the "Why This College?" Essay
https://bemoacademicconsulting.com/blog/why-this-college-essay

College Essay Review Services: Why You Need Them
https://bemoacademicconsulting.com/blog/college-essay-review

College Essay Advisors: Reasons You Need One
https://bemoacademicconsulting.com/blog/college-essay-advisors

College Admissions Consulting: The Secret to Your Success
https://bemoacademicconsulting.com/blog/college-admissions-consulting

Made in the USA
Las Vegas, NV
27 December 2023

83565396R00164